FRIENDSHIP

FRIENDSHIP: THE POWER, PURPOSE,
AND PROVISION OF FRIENDSHIP.

Copyright © 2021 by Love God Greatly Ministry

Permission is granted to print and reproduce this document for the purpose
of completing the *Friendship: The power, purpose, and provision of friendship.*
online Bible study. Please do not alter this document in any way. All rights
reserved. Published in Dallas by Love God Greatly.

Photo source:
unsplash.com

Recipe source:
Cindy, LGG Manadonese Branch

Information and data source:
Joshua Project, https://joshuaproject.net/languages/xmm, accessed February
2021.

Unless otherwise directed in writing by the Publisher, Scripture quotations
are from the NET BIBLE* translation, copyright 2019, by Bible.org. Used by
permission. All rights reserved.

Printed in the United States of America, Library of Congress Cataloging-in-
Publication Data, Printed in the United States of America

26	25	24	23	22	21
6	5	4	3	2	1

WHEN WOMEN ARE
EQUIPPED WITH THE
KNOWLEDGE OF GOD'S
TRUTH, THE WORLD
IS TRANSFORMED ONE
WOMAN AT A TIME.

JOURNAL BELONGS TO

Jaquelyn Perales

DATE

_10 \ 2 \ 22_

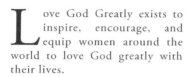

Love God Greatly exists to inspire, encourage, and equip women around the world to love God greatly with their lives.

INSPIRE women to make God's Word a priority in their daily lives through Bible study resources.

ENCOURAGE women in their walks with God through online community and personal accountability.

EQUIP women to grow in their faith so they can effectively reach others for Christ.

We start with a simple Bible reading plan, but it doesn't stop there. Some women gather in homes and churches locally, while others connect online with women across the globe, Whatever the method, we lovingly lock arms and unite for this purpose: to love God greatly with our lives.

At Love God Greatly, you'll find real, authentic women. You'll find women who desire less of each other, and a whole lot more of Jesus. Women who long to know God through His Word because we believe that truth transforms and sets us free. Women who are better together, saturated in God's Word and in community with one another.

Love God Greatly is committed to providing quality Bible study materials and believes finances should never get in the way of a woman being able to participate in one of our studies. All journals are available to download for free from LoveGodGreatly.com.

Our journals and books are also available for sale on Amazon. Search for "Love God Greatly" to see all of our Bible study journals and books.

YOU'LL FIND WOMEN WHO ARE IMPERFECT, YET FORGIVEN.

Love God Greatly is a 501 (C) (3) non-profit organization. Funding for Love God Greatly comes through donations and proceeds from our online Bible study journals and books.

One-hundred percent of proceeds go directly back into supporting Love God Greatly and helping us inspire, encourage, and equip women all over the world with God's Word.

Arm-in-arm and hand-in-hand, let's do this together.

OUR MISSION

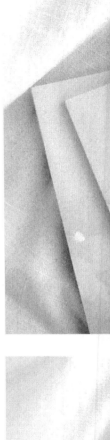

THE NEED

Billions of women around the world don't have access to God's Word in their native language. Those who do, don't have access to women's Bible studies designed and written with them in mind.

THE MISSION

At Love God Greatly, we create Bible studies in 30+ languages. We equip missionaries, ministries, local churches, and women with God's Word at an unprecedented rate by allowing our journals to be downloaded from our international sites at no cost.

Through studying the Bible in their own language with like-minded communities, women are trained and equipped with God's Word.

We believe when women read and apply God's Word to their lives and embrace His unchanging love for them, the world is a better place. We know one woman in God's Word can change a family, a community, and a nation... one woman at a time.

PARTNER WITH US

We would love for you to join us in our mission of giving women all over the world access to God's Word and quality Bible study resources! For any questions or for more information, email us or visit us online. We would love to hear from you!

INFO@LOVEGODGREATLY.COM

LOVEGODGREATLY.COM

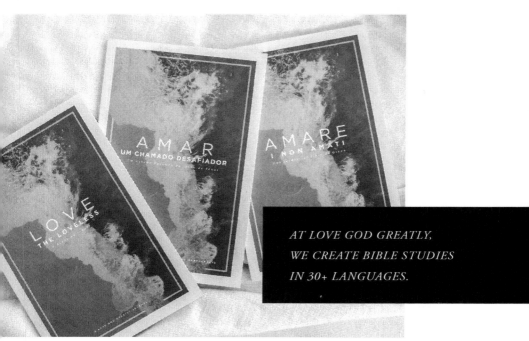

AT LOVE GOD GREATLY,
WE CREATE BIBLE STUDIES
IN 30+ LANGUAGES.

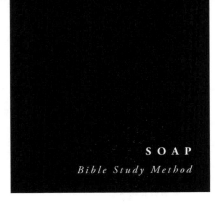

SOAP

Bible Study Method

At Love God Greatly, we believe that the Word of God is living and active. The words of Scripture are powerful and effective and relevant for life in all times and all cultures. In order to interpret the Bible correctly, we need an understanding of the context and culture of the original writings.

As we study the Bible, we use the SOAP Bible Study Method. The acronym stands for Scripture, Observation, Application, and Prayer. It's one thing simply to read Scripture. When you interact with it, intentionally slowing down to reflect, truths start jumping off the page. The SOAP Method allows us to dig deeper into Scripture and see more than we would if we simply read the verses. It allows us not only to be hearers of the Word, but doers as well (Jas 1:22).

YOU WILL NEVER WASTE TIME IN GOD'S WORD. IT IS LIVING, POWERFUL, AND EFFECTIVE, AND HE SPEAKS TO US THROUGH IT.

In this journal, we read a passage of Scripture and then apply the SOAP Method to specific verses. Using this method allows us to glean a greater understanding of Scripture, which allows us to apply it effectively to our lives.

The most important ingredients in the SOAP Method are your interaction with God's Word and your application of it to your life. Take time to study it carefully, discovering the truth of God's character and heart for the world.

Studying God's Word can be challenging and even confusing. We use the SOAP method to help us simplify our study and focus on key passages.

SOAP
Bible Study Method

*Physically write out
the SOAP verses.*

*You'll be amazed at what
God will reveal to you
just by taking the time to
slow down and write out
what you are reading!*

SOAP

WEEK 1 • MONDAY

SCRIPTURE / *Write out the SOAP verses*

Then I heard a loud voice in heaven saying, "The salvation
and the power and the kingdom of our God, and the
ruling authority of his Christ, have now come, because the
accuser of our brothers and sisters, the one who accuses
them day and night before our God, has been thrown
down. Revelation 12:10

But the Lord is faithful, and he will strengthen you and
protect you from the evil one. 2 Thessalonians 3:3

OBSERVATION / *Write 3 – 4 observations*

Loud voice, powerful, all knowing
We are accused day and night, constant struggle
The Lord will help, establish and guard me
He's always there
He's is constant, a protector in my life, guardian

---

*What do you see in the
verses that you're reading?*

*Who is the intended
audience? Is there a
repetition of words?*

*What words stand
out to you?*

INDONESIA

Do you know someone
who could use our Love
God Greatly Bible studies
in the Manadonese
language?

If so, make sure to tell
them all the amazing
Bible study resources we
provide to help equip
them with God's Word!

Tinutuan

(MANADONESE VEGETABLE PORRIDGE)
A TYPICAL BREAKFAST DISH

INGREDIENTS

1 CUP RICE
rinsed, drained

8½ CUPS WATER

½ CUP RED SWEET POTATOES
peeled, diced into ½ inch pieces

½ CUP PUMPKIN
peeled, diced into ½ inch pieces

1½ CUPS SHELLED CORN

¼ CUP SPINACH LEAVES
washed

¼ CUP WATER SPINACH
washed

⅛ CUP BASIL LEAVES
washed

1½ TSP SALT

TOPPINGS & GARNISHES

FRIED SALTED FISH

FRIED TOFU

DABU-DABU
*(Special chili paste, combination of red chili, tomato,
shallot, and other special additional ingredient,
such as shrimp paste, smoked fish, etc.)*

DIRECTIONS

Boil rice along with red sweet potatoes and pumpkin until soft. Stir in the
spinach leaves, water spinach, basil leaves, and corn. Season with salt to
taste. Serve with your choice of toppings and garnishes.

KNOW THESE TRUTHS

GOD LOVES YOU

God's Word says, "For this is the way God loved the world: He gave his one and only Son, so that everyone who believes in him will not perish but have eternal life" (John 3:16).

OUR SIN SEPARATES US FROM GOD

We are all sinners by nature and by choice, and because of this we are separated from God, who is holy. God's Word says, "for all have sinned and fall short of the glory of God" (Rom 3:23).

JESUS DIED SO YOU MIGHT HAVE LIFE

The consequence of sin is death, but God's free gift of salvation is available to us. Jesus took the penalty for our sin when He died on the cross.

God's Word says, "For the payoff of sin is death, but the gift of God is eternal life in Christ Jesus our Lord" (Rom 6:23); "But God demonstrates his own love for us, in that while we were still sinners, Christ died for us" (Rom 5:8).

JESUS LIVES!

Death could not hold Him, and three days after His body was placed in the tomb Jesus rose again, defeating sin and death forever. He lives today in heaven and is preparing a place in eternity for all who believe in Him.

Jesus says, "There are many dwelling places in my Father's house. Otherwise, I would have told you, because I am going away to make ready a place for you. And if I go and make ready a place for you, I will come again and take you to be with me, so that where I am you may be too" (John 14:2–3).

Introduction

On the eve of His crucifixion, Jesus spent time praying for all believers. He prayed that those who placed their faith in Him would remain in Him. The love believers have for one another displays the love the Father has for the Son and for the world.

God's love for the world is the reason He sent His Son, Jesus, to be a sacrifice for our sin. Jesus displayed God's love to the world when He gave His life to save sinners. John 15:13 says, "No one has greater love than this—that one lays down his life for his friends." Jesus' sacrifice was the ultimate example of loving friendship. He loved us so much that He died so we could live with Him forever.

We were designed for community and friendship. God created humanity in the context of a relationship with Himself and with others. Even though going through life alone may seem simpler and free from pain, we were meant to walk in community. We cannot survive without one another. The way we care for and carry one another's burdens shows the world the love of Christ.

We must be on guard from the schemes of the enemy, who is always hoping to destroy our friendships and create dissension and disunity within the body of Christ. In this six-week study, we will walk through what it looks like to have God-honoring friendships and how we can recognize unhealthy and dangerous friendships.

THE WAY WE CARE FOR AND CARRY ONE ANOTHER'S BURDENS SHOWS THE WORLD THE LOVE OF CHRIST.

Friendship is a great provision that God has given us. As we go through life, we need biblical friendships to help us grow in our walk with God, stay steadfast in trials, and combat the schemes of the enemy. Jesus came to befriend and minister to sinners, including us. While our friendships will never be perfect, we can continue to build one another up, asking for and offering forgiveness often, and letting our friendships be a shining witness for the Good News of the gospel of Jesus Christ.

WEEK 1: OUR NEED FOR FRIENDSHIP

Monday / Designed for Friendship
Read: Genesis 1:26-27, 1 John 1:3
SOAP: Genesis 1:27

Tuesday / Created for Community
Read: Genesis 2:18, Ecclesiastes 4:9-12, Matthew 18:20
SOAP: Ecclesiastes 4:9-12

Wednesday / The Impact of Sin on Friendship
Read: Genesis 3:8-13, Genesis 4:6-8
SOAP: Genesis 3:8

Thursday / How Friendship Displays the Gospel
Read: John 13:35, 2 Corinthians 5:18-20
SOAP: John 13:35

Friday / Rooftop Ripping Friends
Read: Mark 2:1-5
SOAP: Mark 2:4

WEEK 2: WHAT IS BIBLICAL FRIENDSHIP?

Monday / Christ-Centered Friendship
Read: Romans 12:1-8, 1 Peter 4:10
SOAP: Romans 12:4-5, 1 Peter 4:10

Tuesday / The Purpose of Biblical Friendships
Read: John 17:20-24
SOAP: John 17:22-23

Wednesday / Thicker than Blood
Read: 1 Samuel 18:1-4, 1 Samuel 20
SOAP: 1 Samuel 18:1-4

Thursday / Lifting Each Other's Load
Read: Galatians 6:1-10
SOAP: Galatians 6:2

Friday / Support in a Broken World
Read: Hebrews 10:24-25, Ruth 1:16-17
SOAP: Hebrews 10:24-25

WEEK 3: THE BLESSING OF FRIENDSHIP

○ *Monday / The Golden Rule*
Read: Luke 6:31-36
SOAP: Luke 6:31

○ *Tuesday / Speak Truth in Love*
Read: Proverbs 27:5-6, Proverbs 28:23, Ephesians 4:15-16
SOAP: Ephesians 4:15-16

○ *Wednesday / A Friend Who is Trustworthy*
Read: Proverbs 11:13
SOAP: Proverbs 11:13

○ *Thursday / Friends Who Sharpen*
Read: Proverbs 27:17, Proverbs 27:9
SOAP: Proverbs 27:17

○ *Friday / The Need for Forgiveness*
Read: Colossians 3:12-14, Ephesians 4:32, Proverbs 17:17
SOAP: Colossians 3:12-14

WEEK 4: DANGEROUS FRIENDSHIPS

○ *Monday / Counterfeit Friendships*
Read: Proverbs 17:9, Romans 16:17-18, 2 Timothy 3:2-5
SOAP: Romans 16:17-18

○ *Tuesday / Threats to Biblical Friendship*
Read: Ephesians 6:12, Proverbs 11:9, Proverbs 11:13
SOAP: Ephesians 6:12

○ *Wednesday / Red Flags*
Read: Proverbs 22:24-25, Proverbs 27:4, 1 Corinthians 15:33, James 4:4-6
SOAP: James 4:4

○ *Thursday / The Impact of Our Words*
Read: Ephesians 4:29, Proverbs 16:24, Proverbs 16:28
SOAP: Ephesians 4:29

○ *Friday / The Importance of Love*
Read: 1 Corinthians 13, Proverbs 12:26
SOAP: 1 Corinthians 13:4-7

WEEK 5: JESUS, A FRIEND OF SINNERS

○ *Monday / Jesus, Friend of Sinners*
Read: John 8:1-11, 1 Timothy 1:15, Luke 5:31-32, Luke 7:34-35
SOAP: 1 Timothy 1:15

○ *Tuesday / Outer Circle, Inner Circle*
Read: Mark 3:13-19, Mark 5:37, Mark 9:2-8
SOAP: Mark 9:2

○ *Wednesday / To Save the Lost*
Read: Luke 15:1-10, Luke 19:1-10
SOAP: Luke 19:10

○ *Thursday / Love Your Neighbor*
Read: Mark 12:30-31, Galatians 5:14-17
SOAP: Galatians 5:14

○ *Friday / Breaking Bread Together*
Read: Acts 2:42-47, Acts 20:7
SOAP: Acts 2:46-47

WEEK 6: THE PROVISION OF FRIENDSHIP

○ *Monday / Jesus, Our Ultimate Best Friend*
Read: 1 Peter 5:6-7
SOAP: 1 Peter 5:7

○ *Tuesday / He Calls You Friend*
Read: John 15:14-17
SOAP: John 15:15

○ *Wednesday / He is Our Faithful Friend*
Read: Proverbs 18:24, Hebrews 13:5-6
SOAP: Proverbs 18:24

○ *Thursday / The Ultimate Sacrifice*
Read: John 15:13, Romans 5:8, Ephesians 5:1-2
SOAP: John 15:13

○ *Friday / Life-Giving Friendships*
Read: Philippians 2:1-18, Romans 12:9-21
SOAP: Romans 12:9-10

YOUR GOALS

Write three goals you would like to focus on as you begin each day and dig into God's Word. Make sure you refer back to these goals throughout the next weeks to help you stay focused. You can do it!

ONE

Becoming more bold in prayer; Not to be afraid to speak out loud my prayer. To not be shy or bashful.

TWO

To sit quietly in the lord for 30 minuetes a
prensense
day. To give him quietness for 30 minutes as worship.

THREE

To walk in obedience everyday; To have a clean heart. A heart that is light and pure. A mind that is filled with Hope and Joy.

READ

Genesis 1:26-27

26 Then God said, "Let us make humankind in our image, after our likeness, so they may rule over the fish of the sea and the birds of the air, over the cattle, and over all the earth, and over all the creatures that move on the earth." 27 God created humankind in his own image, in the image of God he created them, male and female he created them.

1 John 1:3

3 What we have seen and heard we announce to you too, so that you may have fellowship with us (and indeed our fellowship is with the Father and with his Son Jesus Christ).

SOAP / *Genesis 1:27*
SCRIPTURE / *Write out the SOAP verses*

God created humankind in his own image, in the image
of God he created them, male and female he created
them.

OBSERVATION / *Write 3 - 4 observations*

created

Image

Made in his image

Created Humankind

Remind myself that i was made in his likness; to know
that humankind was made with purpose.

Pause an look at everything he created an thank him softly;
admire his work

look at myself an admire the way he molded my
very being. To know i am a work of art.

Thank you father for making humankind
with uniqe beauty. For making us in your
likeness.
I ask that you help me see glimpses of you
in everyone an everything i come across.
To be remind that humankind was no
accident.
we are all a work of art; Each made
diverse from the other.
oh goodness! If i was made in your image
that mean a part of you look's like me.
I am beautiful like you.
Thank you father, lem me not forget
this. Amen.

SOAP

Genesis 1:27

God created humankind in his own image, in the image of God he created them, male and female he created them.

INTO THE TEXT

At the beginning of the Bible, we are given a glimpse into how God created us. We were not made accidentally or unintentionally, but we were made in the image of God. Of everything God made, He designated humanity as those who would rule over creation and show the world who He is. This special status means a lot of different things, but we can know with confidence that God made us to exist in relationship with others.

Our God is triune: three in one. One of the ways we reflect this unique (and often confusing) reality is that we were made to live in community with those who are both different and like us. Even the fact that God created humanity as male and female tells us that He delights in humanity's difference in unity. Relationships with other people are not optional or unnecessary. We need other people because God made us that way. Our relationships might be frustrated by sin—our sin, other people's sin, or the brokenness of the world around us—but relationships themselves are good gifts from God.

PRAYER

Lord, thank You for making me in Your image. Thank You for the relationships in my life. Help me remember how important they are so I can treat other people like they are also made in Your image. Amen.

READ

Genesis 2:18

18 The Lord God said, "It is not good for the man to be alone. I will make a companion for him who corresponds to him."

Ecclesiastes 4:9-12

9 Two people are better than one, because they can reap more benefit from their labor. 10 For if they fall, one will help his companion up, but pity the person who falls down and has no one to help him up. 11 Furthermore, if two lie down together, they can keep each other warm, but how can one person keep warm by himself? 12 Although an assailant may overpower one person, two can withstand him. Moreover, a three-stranded cord is not quickly broken.

Matthew 18:20

20 For where two or three are assembled in my name, I am there among them."

SOAP / *Ecclesiastes 4:9-12*
SCRIPTURE / *Write out the SOAP verses*

_____

_____

_____

_____

_____

_____

_____

_____

_____

_____

_____

_____

_____

_____

_____

_____

_____

_____

_____

_____

_____

OBSERVATION / *Write 3 - 4 observations*

_____

_____

_____

_____

_____

_____

APPLICATION / *Write down 1 - 2 applications*

PRAYER / *Write out a prayer over what you learned*

SOAP

Ecclesiastes 4:9-12

Two people are better than one, because they can reap more benefit from their labor. For if they fall, one will help his companion up, but pity the person who falls down and has no one to help him up. Furthermore, if two lie down together, they can keep each other warm, but how can one person keep warm by himself? Although an assailant may overpower one person, two can withstand him. Moreover, a three-stranded cord is not quickly broken.

INTO THE TEXT

We were created to rely on other people. Sometimes we can be deceived into thinking that before sin entered the world, humans were totally self-sufficient, able to do everything on our own. But we were created, even before sin, as finite creatures: with limited power and abilities. We were created small and weak compared to many of the other creatures God made. From the beginning of the story, we were made to need one another.

This section of Ecclesiastes is on friendship, and it summarizes some of the beautiful benefits of living in community. We can work together to get more accomplished, help each other when we fall, protect each other from the coldness of the world, and we can fight against evil. This is a reminder that our relationships serve a purpose: they aren't just about the good times; they are God's gift to us during the hard times. We need to cultivate relationships that fulfill this purpose by serving one another selflessly and modeling for others what it looks like to care for one another.

PRAYER

God, thank You for this picture of what friendship looks like. Show me the people in my life that I can serve better and with whom I can build a better relationship. Amen.

READ

Genesis 3:8-13

8 Then the man and his wife heard the sound of the LORD God moving about in the orchard at the breezy time of the day, and they hid from the LORD God among the trees of the orchard. 9 But the LORD God called to the man and said to him, "Where are you?" 10 The man replied, "I heard you moving about in the orchard, and I was afraid because I was naked, so I hid." 11 And the LORD God said, "Who told you that you were naked? Did you eat from the tree that I commanded you not to eat from?" 12 The man said, "The woman whom you gave me, she gave me some fruit from the tree and I ate it." 13 So the LORD God said to the woman, "What is this you have done?" And the woman replied, "The serpent tricked me, and I ate."

Genesis 4:6-8

6 Then the LORD said to Cain, "Why are you angry, and why is your expression downcast? 7 Is it not true that if you do what is right, you will be fine? But if you do not do what is right, sin is crouching at the door. It desires to dominate you, but you must subdue it." 8 Cain said to his brother Abel, "Let's go out to the field." While they were in the field, Cain attacked his brother Abel and killed him.

SOAP / *Genesis 3:8*
SCRIPTURE / *Write out the SOAP verses*

_____

_____

_____

_____

_____

_____

_____

_____

_____

_____

_____

_____

_____

_____

_____

_____

_____

_____

_____

_____

_____

OBSERVATION / *Write 3 - 4 observations*

_____

_____

_____

_____

_____

_____

APPLICATION / *Write down 1 - 2 applications*

PRAYER / *Write out a prayer over what you learned*

SOAP

Genesis 3:8

*Then the man and his wife heard the sound of
the LORD God moving about in the orchard at
the breezy time of the day, and they hid from the
LORD God among the trees of the orchard.*

INTO THE TEXT

The entrance of sin into the world impacted humanity
in many ways. The world we live in was fundamentally
changed: the creation that was made good had been
broken and corrupted. Humans were changed: our
relationship with God was broken and our orientation
turned inward. We would consistently make selfish and
sinful choices that hurt ourselves, each other, and God.
Sin impacted our relationships—both vertically and
horizontally. We were separated from God by our sin,
and we were separated from each other.

Even our attempts at community would be stained by sin:
when Adam and Eve hid together from the Lord, they
were working together but in a self-destructive way. Their
relationship with each other would be damaged by sin
(3:12-3:16), but they would also use their relationships
to distance themselves from God. Relationships are a
good gift from God, but we sinful creatures are skilled
at taking good gifts and corrupting them. We can use
our relationships to sin together, especially by gossiping,
excluding others, justifying each other's sin, or relying on
people for things only God can give us.

PRAYER

God, thank You for the gift of relationships. Guard my
heart, God, from the temptation to use my relationships
to sin against others and against You. I don't want to hide
from You, I want to have a relationship with You. Amen.

READ

John 13:35

35 Everyone will know by this that you are my disciples—if you have love for one another."

2 Corinthians 5:18-20

18 And all these things are from God who reconciled us to himself through Christ, and who has given us the ministry of reconciliation. 19 In other words, in Christ God was reconciling the world to himself, not counting people's trespasses against them, and he has given us the message of reconciliation. 20 Therefore we are ambassadors for Christ, as though God were making his plea through us. We plead with you on Christ's behalf, "Be reconciled to God!"

SOAP / *John 13:35*
SCRIPTURE / *Write out the SOAP verses*

_____

_____

_____

_____

_____

_____

_____

_____

_____

_____

_____

_____

_____

_____

_____

_____

_____

_____

OBSERVATION / *Write 3 - 4 observations*

_____

_____

_____

_____

_____

_____

APPLICATION / *Write down 1 - 2 applications*

_____

_____

_____

_____

_____

_____

_____

_____

_____

_____

_____

PRAYER / *Write out a prayer over what you learned*

_____

_____

_____

_____

_____

_____

_____

_____

_____

_____

_____

_____

_____

_____

_____

SOAP

John 13:35

Everyone will know by this that you are my disciples—if you have love for one another.

INTO THE TEXT

We witness to the world with more than our words. Our words are important: we need to share the gospel with a weary world by telling them the truth. Jesus did more than that. He lived His life in a way that invited people to follow Him. He created a community of people that lived such different lives that others were confused, intrigued, and sometimes angry. As we carry a strange and radical message into the world, we can show the world its true meaning by displaying love for one another.

We have been commissioned by God to reconcile relationships. In a world corrupted by sin, self-sacrificial love is uncommon. Our individual relationships with one another, our churches, our small groups and Bible studies, our communities—all these relationships can attest to the power of the gospel. We are not capable, on our own, of the kind of love that will show people we are Jesus' disciples. With the power of the Holy Spirit working in our lives, though, we can show the world a type of relationship they have never seen before.

PRAYER

God, work in me! Make me more like Your Son, someone who showed overwhelming love to the world. Help me have the kind of love for my brothers and sisters that will show them who You are. Amen.

READ

Mark 2:1-5

Now after some days, when he returned to Capernaum, the news spread that he was at home. 2 So many gathered that there was no longer any room, not even by the door, and he preached the word to them. 3 Some people came bringing to him a paralytic, carried by four of them. 4 When they were not able to bring him in because of the crowd, they removed the roof above Jesus. Then, after tearing it out, they lowered the stretcher the paralytic was lying on. 5 When Jesus saw their faith, he said to the paralytic, "Son, your sins are forgiven."

SOAP / *Mark 2:4*
SCRIPTURE / *Write out the SOAP verses*

_____

_____

_____

_____

_____

_____

_____

_____

_____

_____

_____

_____

_____

_____

_____

_____

_____

_____

_____

_____

OBSERVATION / *Write 3 - 4 observations*

_____

_____

_____

_____

_____

_____

APPLICATION / *Write down 1 - 2 applications*

_____

_____

_____

_____

_____

_____

_____

_____

_____

_____

_____

PRAYER / *Write out a prayer over what you learned*

_____

_____

_____

_____

_____

_____

_____

_____

_____

_____

_____

_____

_____

_____

_____

SOAP

Mark 2:4

*When they were not able to bring him in because
of the crowd, they removed the roof above
Jesus. Then, after tearing it out, they lowered
the stretcher the paralytic was lying on.*

INTO THE TEXT

What does it look like to be a good friend? The friends in this passage are a powerful example of what it means to be a true friend. These friends knew their friend's suffering and sought healing from Jesus. When the crowds of people threatened to prevent their friends' healing, they did not give up. They found a creative solution that displayed great faith. When it says Jesus saw their faith, it means both that Jesus saw the faith of these hardworking friends and that He saw the faith of the paralytic.

It takes faith to fight for your friends, and it takes faith to let them fight for you. When our friends are suffering, we need to be the kind of friends who will fight to seek God's comfort and healing. When we are suffering, we often need to cease our striving and let our friends bear our burdens with us. We were not intended to be self-sufficient; we were created with a need for relationships that will point us back to God.

PRAYER

God, show me who in my life is hurting. Give me the resources to serve them well and give me the right words to comfort them and glorify You. Amen.

1. *How are we designed for friendship and community? How should we live knowing we are designed this way?*

....

....

....

2. *In what ways does living in community offer benefits to our lives and the lives of others?*

....

....

....

3. *How did sin entering the world affect our ability to live in community with God? How did this event affect our ability to live in community with others?*

....

....

....

4. *How does our love for our friends and other believers in Christ display God's love to the world?*

....

....

....

5. *How can we live out the ministry of reconciliation and be an example of Christ's love to the world?*

....

....

....

The *glory* you gave
to me I have given
to them, that they
may be one just
as we are one—I in
them and you in
me—that they may
be _completely_ one, so
that the world will
know that you sent
me, and you have
loved *them* just as
you have _loved me_.

John 17:22-23

*Write down your prayer requests
and praises for this week.*

....

....

....

....

....

....

....

....

....

....

....

....

WEEKLY CHALLENGE

*What can you do this week to spur your friends on to love and good works? This week,
spend time with your friends, intentionally encouraging and challenging one another
with God's Word.*

....

....

....

....

....

....

....

....

READ

Romans 12:1-8

Therefore I exhort you, brothers and sisters, by the mercies of God, to present your bodies as a sacrifice—alive, holy, and pleasing to God—which is your reasonable service. 2 Do not be conformed to this present world, but be transformed by the renewing of your mind, so that you may test and approve what is the will of God—what is good and well-pleasing and perfect. 3 For by the grace given to me I say to every one of you not to think more highly of yourself than you ought to think, but to think with sober discernment, as God has distributed to each of you a measure of faith. 4 For just as in one body we have many members, and not all the members serve the same function, 5 so we who are many are one body in Christ, and individually we are members who belong to one another. 6 And we have different gifts according to the grace given to us. If the gift is prophecy, that individual must use it in proportion to his faith. 7 If it is service, he must serve; if it is teaching, he must teach; 8 if it is exhortation, he must exhort; if it is contributing, he must do so with sincerity; if it is leadership, he must do so with diligence; if it is showing mercy, he must do so with cheerfulness.

1 Peter 4:10

10 Just as each one has received a gift, use it to serve one another as good stewards of the varied grace of God.

SOAP / *Romans 12:4-5, 1 Peter 4:10*
SCRIPTURE / *Write out the SOAP verses*

_____

_____

_____

_____

_____

_____

_____

_____

_____

_____

_____

_____

_____

_____

_____

_____

_____

_____

_____

_____

OBSERVATION / *Write 3 - 4 observations*

_____

_____

_____

_____

_____

_____

APPLICATION / *Write down 1 - 2 applications*

PRAYER / *Write out a prayer over what you learned*

SOAP

Romans 12:4-5

For just as in one body we have many members, and not all the members serve the same function, so we who are many are one body in Christ, and individually we are members who belong to one another.

1 Peter 4:10

Just as each one has received a gift, use it to serve one another as good stewards of the varied grace of God.

INTO THE TEXT

Sometimes we may wish that our friends were more like us—that they shared our same interests, felt the same way we feel, agreed with us about everything—but it is very good news that we are not all the same. We can strengthen and encourage one another in unique ways because we all have different gifts. Someone may have strong faith that another friend leans on when she struggles to trust God. Someone else may understand Scripture clearly and can explain it to her friends. These gifts are not for us to enjoy individually, they are given to us by God so that we can serve one another and be more unified together in Christ.

We belong to one another, and so we have no right to use our own gifts for solely our own advantage. Friendship can help us stop competing or comparing gifts, seeking the spotlight for ourselves, or diminishing someone else's gifts. We are on the same team, and our gifts are meant to complement each other.

PRAYER

God, show me how to use my gifts to serve the body of Christ. Show me how to encourage my friends in their gifts and truly celebrate them instead of competing or comparing. Help us show the world what it means to be united in You. Amen.

READ

John 17:20-24

20 "I am not praying only on their behalf, but also on behalf of those who believe in me through their testimony, 21 that they will all be one, just as you, Father, are in me and I am in you. I pray that they will be in us, so that the world will believe that you sent me. 22 The glory you gave to me I have given to them, that they may be one just as we are one— 23 I in them and you in me—that they may be completely one, so that the world will know that you sent me, and you have loved them just as you have loved me. 24 "Father, I want those you have given me to be with me where I am, so that they can see my glory that you gave me because you loved me before the creation of the world.

SOAP / *John 17:22-23*
SCRIPTURE / *Write out the SOAP verses*

_____

_____

_____

_____

_____

_____

_____

_____

_____

_____

_____

_____

_____

_____

_____

_____

_____

_____

_____

_____

OBSERVATION / *Write 3 - 4 observations*

_____

_____

_____

_____

_____

_____

APPLICATION / *Write down 1 - 2 applications*

PRAYER / *Write out a prayer over what you learned*

SOAP

John 17:22-23

The glory you gave to me I have given to them,
that they may be one just as we are one—I in them
and you in me—that they may be completely one,
so that the world will know that you sent me, and
you have loved them just as you have loved me.

INTO THE TEXT

The world has a lot of experience with unhealthy relationships. The unbelievers around us have seen friendships that consisted of gossip and exclusion, friends that only helped one another when they expected something in return, and friendships that were filled with arguing and dissension. Part of our witness to the watching world is showing them something different. When our friendships are defined by sacrificial love, they point to God's sacrificial love for the world.

The Father sent the Son into the world to show real love, and He sends us with a similar mission. When we cultivate relationships defined by honesty, grace, and service, we just might catch the attention of people hungry for that kind of connection. Finding it is rare, and we have an opportunity to not only model those relationships for others, but to extend that friendship to them. When we are frustrated by our failed attempts at evangelizing, maybe we need to take a step back and ask how we can be a good friend to others. Our love for each other—and our inclusion of outsiders—may open opportunities to point people to the One who has sent us.

PRAYER

God, bring people into my life that I can share Your love with! Strengthen my friendships, so they can point people to Your love for the world. Amen.

WEEK 2
Wednesday

READ

1 Samuel 18:1-4

When David had finished talking with Saul, Jonathan and David became bound together in close friendship. Jonathan loved David as much as he did his own life. 2 Saul retained David on that day and did not allow him to return to his father's house. 3 Jonathan made a covenant with David, for he loved him as much as he did his own life. 4 Jonathan took off the robe he was wearing and gave it to David, along with the rest of his gear including his sword, his bow, and even his belt.

1 Samuel 20

David fled from Naioth in Ramah. He came to Jonathan and asked, "What have I done? What is my offense? How have I sinned before your father, that he is seeking my life?" 2 Jonathan said to him, "By no means are you going to die! My father does nothing large or small without making me aware of it. Why would my father hide this matter from me? It just won't happen!" 3 Taking an oath, David again said, "Your father is very much aware of the fact that I have found favor with you, and he has thought, 'Don't let Jonathan know about this, or he will be upset.' But as surely as the LORD lives and you live, there is about one step between me and death!" 4 Jonathan replied to David, "Tell me what I can do for you." 5 David said to Jonathan, "Tomorrow is the new moon, and I am certainly expected to join the king for a meal. You must send me away so I can hide in the field until the third evening from now. 6 If your father happens to miss me, you should say, 'David urgently requested me to let him go to his town Bethlehem, for there is an annual sacrifice there for his entire family.' 7 If he should then say, 'That's fine,' then your servant is safe. But if he becomes very angry, be assured that he has decided to harm me. 8 You must be loyal to your servant, for you have made a covenant with your servant in the LORD's name. If I am guilty, you yourself kill me! Why bother taking me to your father?" 9 Jonathan said, "Far be it from you to suggest this! If I were at all aware that my father had decided to harm you,

1 Samuel 20 (Continued)

wouldn't I tell you about it?" 10 David said to Jonathan, "Who will tell me if your father answers you harshly?" 11 Jonathan said to David, "Come on. Let's go out to the field." When the two of them had gone out into the field, 12 Jonathan said to David, "The LORD God of Israel is my witness! I will feel out my father about this time the day after tomorrow. If he is favorably inclined toward David, will I not then send word to you and let you know? 13 But if my father intends to do you harm, may the LORD do all this and more to Jonathan, if I don't let you know and send word to you, so you can go safely on your way. May the LORD be with you, as he was with my father. 14 While I am still alive, extend to me the loyalty of the LORD, or else I will die. 15 Don't ever cut off your loyalty to my family, not even when the LORD has cut off every one of David's enemies from the face of the earth 16 and called David's enemies to account." So Jonathan made a covenant with the house of David. 17 Jonathan once again took an oath with David, because he loved him. In fact Jonathan loved him as much as he did his own life. 18 Jonathan said to him, "Tomorrow is the new moon, and you will be missed, for your seat will be empty. 19 On the third day you should go down quickly and come to the place where you hid yourself the day this all started. Stay near the stone Ezel. 20 I will shoot three arrows near it, as though I were shooting at a target. 21 When I send a boy after them, I will say, 'Go and find the arrows.' If I say to the boy, 'Look, the arrows are on this side of you; get them,' then come back. For as surely as the LORD lives, you will be safe and there will be no problem. 22 But if I say to the boy, 'Look, the arrows are on the other side of you,' then get away. For in that case the LORD has sent you away. 23 With regard to the matter that you and I discussed, the LORD is the witness between us forever." 24 So David hid in the field. When the new moon came, the king sat down to eat his meal. 25 The king sat down in his usual place by the wall, with Jonathan opposite him and Abner at his side. But David's place was vacant. 26 However, Saul said nothing about it that day, for he thought, "Something has happened to make him ceremonially unclean. Yes, he must be unclean." 27 But the next morning, the second day of the new moon, David's

1 Samuel 20 (Continued)

place was still vacant. So Saul said to his son Jonathan, "Why has Jesse's son not come to the meal yesterday or today?" 28 Jonathan replied to Saul, "David urgently requested that he be allowed to go to Bethlehem. 29 He said, 'Permit me to go, for we are having a family sacrifice in the town, and my brother urged me to be there. So now, if I have found favor with you, let me go to see my brothers.' For that reason he has not come to the king's table." 30 Saul became angry with Jonathan and said to him, "You stupid traitor! Don't I realize that to your own disgrace and to the disgrace of your mother's nakedness you have chosen this son of Jesse? 31 For as long as this son of Jesse is alive on the earth, you and your kingdom will not be established. Now, send some men and bring him to me. For he is as good as dead!" 32 Jonathan responded to his father Saul, "Why should he be put to death? What has he done?" 33 Then Saul threw his spear at Jonathan in order to strike him down. So Jonathan was convinced that his father had decided to kill David. 34 Jonathan got up from the table enraged. He did not eat any food on that second day of the new moon, for he was upset that his father had humiliated David. 35 The next morning Jonathan, along with a young servant, went out to the field to meet David. 36 He said to his servant, "Run, find the arrows that I am about to shoot." As the servant ran, Jonathan shot the arrow beyond him. 37 When the servant came to the place where Jonathan had shot the arrow, Jonathan called out to the servant, "Isn't the arrow farther beyond you?" 38 Jonathan called out to the servant, "Hurry! Go faster! Don't delay!" Jonathan's servant retrieved the arrow and came back to his master. 39 (Now the servant did not understand any of this. Only Jonathan and David knew what was going on.) 40 Then Jonathan gave his equipment to the servant who was with him. He said to him, "Go, take these things back to the town." 41 When the servant had left, David got up from beside the mound, knelt with his face to the ground, and bowed three times. Then they kissed each other and they both wept, especially David. 42 Jonathan said to David, "Go in peace, for the two of us have sworn together in the name of the LORD saying, 'The LORD will be between me and you and between my descendants and your descendants forever.'"

SOAP / *1 Samuel 18:1-4*
SCRIPTURE / *Write out the SOAP verses*

_____

_____

_____

_____

_____

_____

_____

_____

_____

_____

_____

_____

_____

_____

_____

_____

_____

_____

_____

_____

OBSERVATION / *Write 3 - 4 observations*

_____

_____

_____

_____

_____

_____

APPLICATION / *Write down 1 - 2 applications*

·

PRAYER / *Write out a prayer over what you learned*

SOAP

1 Samuel 18:1-4

When David had finished talking with Saul, Jonathan and David became bound together in close friendship. Jonathan loved David as much as he did his own life. Saul retained David on that day and did not allow him to return to his father's house. Jonathan made a covenant with David, for he loved him as much as he did his own life. Jonathan took off the robe he was wearing and gave it to David, along with the rest of his gear, including his sword, his bow, and even his belt.

INTO THE TEXT

Few of us would think about making a covenant with our friends! David and Jonathan are a good example of how strong a friendship can be when it is rooted in mutual love for God. Even when Jonathan's father wanted to kill David, Jonathan was loyal to his friend. It might surprise many of us to think that our faith could ask us to be more loyal to our friends than to our family! The New Testament takes this example even further. The people of God are no longer defined by being born into the ethnic people of Israel, but by acceptance into the family of God.

Our friendships with believers should look different than our other relationships because we share a common purpose. We are called to spend our lives pointing to the kingdom of God, glorifying Him with our lives, and sharing the Good News of the gospel with a weary world. Our allegiance to God may cause tension in our families, like it did for Jonathan, but he had the gift of a godly friend. We can find comfort in the everlasting family we have been accepted into.

PRAYER

God, thank You for making me a part of Your family! Help me protect and fight for my friends the way Jonathan did for David. Amen.

READ

Galatians 6:1-10

Brothers and sisters, if a person is discovered in some sin, you who are spiritual restore such a person in a spirit of gentleness. Pay close attention to yourselves, so that you are not tempted too. 2 Carry one another's burdens, and in this way you will fulfill the law of Christ. 3 For if anyone thinks he is something when he is nothing, he deceives himself. 4 Let each one examine his own work. Then he can take pride in himself and not compare himself with someone else. 5 For each one will carry his own load. 6 Now the one who receives instruction in the word must share all good things with the one who teaches it. 7 Do not be deceived. God will not be made a fool. For a person will reap what he sows, 8 because the person who sows to his own flesh will reap corruption from the flesh, but the one who sows to the Spirit will reap eternal life from the Spirit. 9 So we must not grow weary in doing good, for in due time we will reap, if we do not give up. 10 So then, whenever we have an opportunity, let us do good to all people, and especially to those who belong to the family of faith.

SOAP / *Galatians 6:2*
SCRIPTURE / *Write out the SOAP verses*

_____

_____

_____

_____

_____

_____

_____

_____

_____

_____

_____

_____

_____

_____

_____

_____

_____

_____

_____

_____

OBSERVATION / *Write 3 - 4 observations*

_____

_____

_____

_____

_____

_____

APPLICATION / *Write down 1 - 2 applications*

PRAYER / *Write out a prayer over what you learned*

SOAP

Galatians 6:2

*Carry one another's burdens, and in this
way you will fulfill the law of Christ.*

INTO THE TEXT

Our relationship with God is not private. Sometimes we can tend to picture "me and Jesus against the world," as if the only thing that really matters is our personal relationship with Christ. That relationship is incredibly important, but as Paul points out in Galatians 6:2, that personal relationship comes with some requirements: fulfilling the law of Christ. Jesus spent His years of earthly ministry teaching people about Himself and His Father, but He also spent a lot of time teaching people how to treat one another and how to live their lives. He came with ethical imperatives, including the one in this verse: carry one another's burdens!

Our relationship with God should flow into the way we treat others, especially others in the family of God. We all have burdens to bear, whether it be suffering, loss, disappointment, frustration, or fear. Perhaps our greatest gift to one another may be our willingness to help carry the load. When we are tempted to despair, it is the comfort of our friends that can help us have faith. When we follow this command to carry each other's burdens, we show that we believe what Jesus said and what He did: bearing the burden of sin on our behalf.

PRAYER

Lord, thank You for bearing my greatest burden for me! Show me how to serve and comfort the suffering people in my life. Amen.

READ

Hebrews 10:24-25

24 And let us take thought of how to spur one another on to love and good works, 25 not abandoning our own meetings, as some are in the habit of doing, but encouraging each other, and even more so because you see the day drawing near.

Ruth 1:16-17

16 But Ruth replied, "Stop urging me to abandon you! For wherever you go, I will go. Wherever you live, I will live. Your people will become my people, and your God will become my God. 17 Wherever you die, I will die—and there I will be buried. May the Lord punish me severely if I do not keep my promise! Only death will be able to separate me from you!"

SOAP / *Hebrews 10:24-25*
SCRIPTURE / *Write out the SOAP verses*

OBSERVATION / *Write 3 - 4 observations*

APPLICATION / *Write down 1 - 2 applications*

PRAYER / *Write out a prayer over what you learned*

SOAP

Hebrews 10:24-25

And let us take thought of how to spur one another on to love and good works, not abandoning our own meetings, as some are in the habit of doing, but encouraging each other, and even more so because you see the day drawing near.

INTO THE TEXT

Bearing each other's burdens is difficult work. Sometimes we do this literally: when a friend is moving, you might offer to help carry heavy furniture and boxes up and down stairs, into a moving truck, and unload everything at their destination. Sometimes these burdens are emotional or spiritual, like grief, fear, mental illness, or questions of faith. The work of bearing burdens can be tiring, and many of us face the temptation to give up. When we feel that we've already done so much for our friends by bearing physical, tangible burdens, we feel tempted to give up on their emotional or spiritual burdens.

But a good friend does not abandon their relationships. Just as the church is instructed to keep meeting even when it is difficult, and just as Ruth was faithful to Naomi even when she was not under any obligation to stay with her, we are called to support our friends. We can encourage one another to love God more truly and serve Him more faithfully by our persistent friendship. When it would be easier to give up on someone is exactly the crucial moment to show that our love comes from God, not ourselves. He is the source of our faithfulness to one another.

PRAYER

God, help me love my friends well. Show me who needs my support right now and show me how I can provide it with Your strength. Amen.

1. How are believers in Christ all part of one body?

....

....

....

2. Why do you think God gave each of us a different function in the body of Christ? How does this help the body of Christ grow?

....

....

....

3. Why is it important to carry one another's burdens? How can you carry the burdens of your friends?

....

....

....

4. Is carrying the burdens of others the same as solving their problems? How are the two different?

....

....

....

5. How does unity in the body of Christ display God's love for His Son?

....

....

....

And to
all these
virtues
add love,
which is
the perfect
bond.

Colossians 3:14

PRAY

*Write down your prayer requests
and praises for this week.*

....

....

....

....

....

....

....

....

....

....

....

....

WEEKLY CHALLENGE

*Make a commitment to be a completely trustworthy friend this week. If you slip and
gossip about someone or share something you shouldn't, work intentionally to build
habits that foster love and trust in friendship instead of dissension.*

....

....

....

....

....

....

....

....

READ

Luke 6:31-36

31 Treat others in the same way that you would want them to treat you. 32 "If you love those who love you, what credit is that to you? For even sinners love those who love them. 33 And if you do good to those who do good to you, what credit is that to you? Even sinners do the same. 34 And if you lend to those from whom you hope to be repaid, what credit is that to you? Even sinners lend to sinners, so that they may be repaid in full. 35 But love your enemies, and do good, and lend, expecting nothing back. Then your reward will be great, and you will be sons of the Most High, because he is kind to ungrateful and evil people. 36 Be merciful, just as your Father is merciful.

SOAP / *Luke 6:31*
SCRIPTURE / *Write out the SOAP verses*

_____

_____

_____

_____

_____

_____

_____

_____

_____

_____

_____

_____

_____

_____

_____

_____

_____

_____

_____

_____

_____

OBSERVATION / *Write 3 - 4 observations*

_____

_____

_____

_____

_____

_____

APPLICATION / *Write down 1 - 2 applications*

PRAYER / *Write out a prayer over what you learned*

SOAP

Luke 6:31

*Treat others in the same way that you
would want them to treat you.*

INTO THE TEXT

Some of us are keeping score of our friendships in our heads: points for kindness and generosity, negative points for a harsh word or an unfulfilled promise. We will show up for a friend in need if they've done the same for us, but not if we think they don't deserve our help. We can feel like a friend "owes us" because of what we've done for them. None of these ways of thinking is the way Jesus calls us to treat others.

The world of the first century is not that different from our world today in this regard: we expect reciprocity. If someone is kind to you, you show kindness in return. If someone hurts you, you hurt them back. Jesus' command is just as radical today as it was then: give love freely, not expecting anything in return. Instead of choosing friends based on what they can give us— by their wealth, power, or influence—we are free to love others without strings attached. God was gracious with us when we deserved His wrath, and we can show the world this redemptive truth by treating others well without any expectation that they will return the favor.

PRAYER

God, thank You for treating me better than I deserve! Give me the grace to love others the same way. Amen.

READ

Proverbs 27:5-6

Better is open rebuke than hidden love. 6 Faithful are the wounds of a friend, but the kisses of an enemy are excessive.

Proverbs 28:23

The one who reproves another will in the end find more favor than the one who flatters with the tongue.

Ephesians 4:15-16

15 But practicing the truth in love, we will in all things grow up into Christ, who is the head. 16 From him the whole body grows, fitted and held together through every supporting ligament. As each one does its part, the body builds itself up in love.

SOAP / *Ephesians 4:15-16*
SCRIPTURE / *Write out the SOAP verses*

_____

_____

_____

_____

_____

_____

_____

_____

_____

_____

_____

_____

_____

_____

_____

_____

_____

_____

_____

OBSERVATION / *Write 3 - 4 observations*

_____

_____

_____

_____

_____

_____

_____

APPLICATION / *Write down 1 - 2 applications*

PRAYER / *Write out a prayer over what you learned*

SOAP

Ephesians 4:15-16

But practicing the truth in love, we will in all things grow up into Christ, who is the head. From him the whole body grows, fitted and held together through every supporting ligament. As each one does its part, the body grows in love.

INTO THE TEXT

Some of us are more interested in being nice than being kind. We want everyone to like us, so we put on a fake smile and pretend that everything is fine even when it is not. We avoid controversy or hard conversations because we're afraid of upsetting anyone, and we smooth over disagreements without getting to the root of the problem. We love being liked more than we love the people in our lives.

This is not real love. Paul encouraged the Ephesian Christians to practice truth in love, knowing that real relationships are built on honesty and love. Without truth, our love is superficial and flimsy, easily broken by difficulties. Without love, our truth is so harsh that it prevents reconciliation. Instead, we are called to practice both together: speaking the truth boldly because we love the ones who need to hear it. As we each do our part to build stronger relationships, the whole body of Christ better exhibits the love and the truth at the heart of our faith.

PRAYER

God, help me love others more than I love being liked. Give me opportunities and the strength to practice truth in love in my relationships this week. Amen.

READ

Proverbs 11:13

The one who goes about slandering others reveals secrets,
but the one who is trustworthy conceals a matter.

SOAP / *Proverbs 11:13*
SCRIPTURE / *Write out the SOAP verses*

_____

_____

_____

_____

_____

_____

_____

_____

_____

_____

_____

_____

_____

_____

_____

_____

_____

_____

_____

_____

_____

OBSERVATION / *Write 3 - 4 observations*

_____

_____

_____

_____

_____

_____

APPLICATION / *Write down 1 - 2 applications*

PRAYER / *Write out a prayer over what you learned*

SOAP

Proverbs 11:13

*The one who goes about slandering others reveals secrets,
but the one who is trustworthy conceals a matter.*

INTO THE TEXT

This is one of our enemy's most common strategies: taking good gifts of God and twisting them into tools of destruction. Gossip is one such perversion, because it takes the good gift of bonding over sharing stories and turns it into a powerful force for destroying relationships. Many of us have experienced the bonds that can be built when a group of friends or coworkers has fresh gossip. We all want to be in on the secret and share juicy information with a friend. Gossip can cause more damage than we realize.

Relationships are built on trust, and we destroy that trust when we gossip. We also harm the relationships of the ones we gossip with because we display that we cannot be trusted to honor our friends. Friendships built on gossip are mirages: they look real, but they disappear the second we try to rely upon them. True friendships require knowing that we can depend on each other to hold our private fears and hopes in confidence, because we love the other person enough to prioritize their trust over the momentary excitement of gossiping.

PRAYER

God, convict my heart the next time I am tempted to gossip. Show me how to build real and lasting relationships of trust. Amen.

.

READ

Proverbs 27:17

As iron sharpens iron, so a person sharpens his friend.

Proverbs 27:9

Ointment and incense make the heart rejoice, likewise the sweetness of one's friend from sincere counsel.

SOAP / *Proverbs 27:17*
SCRIPTURE / *Write out the SOAP verses*

OBSERVATION / *Write 3 - 4 observations*

APPLICATION / *Write down 1 - 2 applications*

PRAYER / *Write out a prayer over what you learned*

SOAP

Proverbs 27:17

As iron sharpens iron, so a person sharpens his friend.

INTO THE TEXT

If you've ever cut your hand with a dull knife, you know how important it is for a tool to be sharp. A dull knife does not fulfill its intended purpose (cutting the right object with precision) and instead causes pain. Iron can be sharpened with another piece of iron. One tool that was functioning the way it was intended was used to take a dull tool and restore it to its rightful condition. This is what our friendships should do: restore each other to functioning the way we were intended.

Since the introduction of sin into the world, nothing has functioned the way it should, including humans. Instead of being oriented towards God, we have turned inward to ourselves. We are consumed in selfish destruction because we are not operating the way our Creator intended. Our friends can be instruments of God's grace in our lives to restore us to our rightful condition. This happens when we kindly rebuke one another over sin in our lives, encourage one another, and help one other grow in our gifts.

PRAYER

God, thank You for the gift of friends! Help me cultivate the kind of relationships that sharpen me in my faith. Show me how I can be that kind of friend to the people in my life. Amen.

READ

Colossians 3:12-14

12 Therefore, as the elect of God, holy and dearly loved, clothe yourselves with a heart of mercy, kindness, humility, gentleness, and patience, 13 bearing with one another and forgiving one another, if someone happens to have a complaint against anyone else. Just as the LORD has forgiven you, so you also forgive others. 14 And to all these virtues add love, which is the perfect bond.

Ephesians 4:32

32 Instead, be kind to one another, compassionate, forgiving one another, just as God in Christ also forgave you.

Proverbs 17:17

A friend loves at all times, and a relative is born to help in adversity.

SOAP / *Colossians 3:12-14*
SCRIPTURE / *Write out the SOAP verses*

_____

_____

_____

_____

_____

_____

_____

_____

_____

_____

_____

_____

_____

_____

_____

_____

_____

_____

_____

_____

_____

OBSERVATION / *Write 3 - 4 observations*

_____

_____

_____

_____

_____

_____

APPLICATION / *Write down 1 - 2 applications*

PRAYER / *Write out a prayer over what you learned*

SOAP

Colossians 3:12-14

Therefore, as the elect of God, holy and dearly loved, clothe yourselves with a heart of mercy, kindness, humility, gentleness, and patience, bearing with one another and forgiving one another, if someone happens to have a complaint against anyone else. Just as the LORD has forgiven you, so you also forgive others. And to all these virtues add love, which is the perfect bond.

INTO THE TEXT

All our friendships will require forgiveness at some point or another. We make mistakes, we miscommunicate, we even sin against each other intentionally. The mark of a good friendship is not that friends never argue but that they seek reconciliation. That might sound simple, but forgiveness is rarely easy. It means we will have to take the weight of another person's sin on ourselves, to deal with their mistakes and choose to maintain a relationship with them anyway. It means we cannot hold past sins against them or keep a tally of every wrong thing they've ever done.

Then comes the most radical part of this command: we are instructed to forgive others as God has forgiven us. God forgave us when we had done nothing to deserve forgiveness, and it cost Him dearly to secure reconciliation with us. That kind of forgiveness is inconceivable to many of us who have only ever known relationships that are always teetering on the brink of another blow-out fight, rehashing old sins. But that forgiveness is necessary. It will look foreign to the rest of the world—a witness to the difference God makes in our lives.

PRAYER

Lord, give me the grace to offer forgiveness to people who have wronged me. Help me understand how You have forgiven me so I can forgive others. Amen.

REFLECT
WEEK 3

1. *Why is it important for us to treat those who hurt us with kindness and grace?*

....

....

....

2. *What does it mean to practice speaking truth in love? Why is it often a challenge to join truth and love together? Why is it important to practice speaking truth with love?*

....

....

....

3. *What does it mean to clothe yourself with a heart of mercy, kindness, humility, gentleness, and patience?*

....

....

....

4. *Why is forgiveness important in friendship? When has a friend's forgiveness blessed you?*

....

....

....

5. *What about love makes it the perfect bond of friendship?*

....

....

....

Love is patient,
love is kind,
it is not envious.
Love does not brag,
it is not puffed up.
It is not rude,
it is not self-serving,
it is not easily
angered or resentful.
It is not glad
about injustice, but
rejoices in the truth.
It bears all things,
believes all things,
hopes all things,
endures all things.

1 Corinthians 13:4-7

PRAY

Write down your prayer requests
and praises for this week.

....

....

....

....

....

....

....

....

....

....

....

....

WEEKLY CHALLENGE

As we seek to develop and foster biblical friendships, we have a very real enemy who
wants to destroy our work. Spiritual warfare is real and we need to be on guard in
our relationships. This week, write out a specific prayer list for your friends, asking
God to guard your relationships and theirs from spiritual attack.

....

....

....

....

....

....

....

READ

Proverbs 17:9

The one who forgives an offense seeks love, but whoever repeats a matter separates close friends.

Romans 16:17-18

17 Now I urge you, brothers and sisters, to watch out for those who create dissensions and obstacles contrary to the teaching that you learned. Avoid them! 18 For these are the kind who do not serve our LORD Christ, but their own appetites. By their smooth talk and flattery they deceive the minds of the naive.

2 Timothy 3:2-5

2 For people will be lovers of themselves, lovers of money, boastful, arrogant, blasphemers, disobedient to parents, ungrateful, unholy, 3 unloving, irreconcilable, slanderers, without self-control, savage, opposed to what is good, 4 treacherous, reckless, conceited, loving pleasure rather than loving God. 5 They will maintain the outward appearance of religion but will have repudiated its power. So avoid people like these.

SOAP / *Romans 16:17-18*
SCRIPTURE / *Write out the SOAP verses*

_____

_____

_____

_____

_____

_____

_____

_____

_____

_____

_____

_____

_____

_____

_____

_____

_____

_____

_____

_____

OBSERVATION / *Write 3 - 4 observations*

_____

_____

_____

_____

_____

_____

APPLICATION / *Write down 1 - 2 applications*

_____
_____
_____
_____
_____
_____
_____
_____
_____
_____
_____

PRAYER / *Write out a prayer over what you learned*

_____
_____
_____
_____
_____
_____
_____
_____
_____
_____
_____
_____
_____
_____
_____

SOAP

Romans 16:17-18

Now I urge you, brothers and sisters, to watch out for those who create dissensions and obstacles contrary to the teaching that you learned. Avoid them! For these are the kind who do not serve our LORD Christ, but their own appetites. By their smooth talk and flattery they deceive the minds of the naive.

INTO THE TEXT

The early church and our current churches face a similar problem: people who are only interested in serving themselves. Dissension and disunity are the common result of people who are not interested in working toward a common goal but instead work toward fulfilling their own desires. These people may look the part and say all the right things, but underneath the veneer, they are only interested in their own status or power.

We may have friends who operate the same way by putting on a false face of friendship without any real substance. While this passage warns the church against false teaching, it also points to a general human tendency to serve our own interests above all else—and to use deceptive speech to hide it. Just as we do not want to be the kind of friends who seek reciprocity—I'll extend kindness just as far as I know you can repay it—we also want to guard ourselves against friends like this. These false friends can cause dissension among real friends by gossiping and inciting conflict. We can ask God for wisdom to guard our friendships against discord and superficiality.

PRAYER

God, help me to accurately assess my relationships and bring my concerns to You. Give me good friends who speak truth. Amen.

READ

Ephesians 6:12

12 For our struggle is not against flesh and blood, but against the rulers, against the powers, against the world rulers of this darkness, against the spiritual forces of evil in the heavens.

Proverbs 11:9

With his speech the godless person destroys his neighbor, but by knowledge the righteous will be delivered.

Proverbs 11:13

The one who goes about slandering others reveals secrets, but the one who is trustworthy conceals a matter.

SOAP / *Ephesians 6:12*
SCRIPTURE / *Write out the SOAP verses*

_____
_____
_____
_____
_____
_____
_____
_____
_____
_____
_____
_____
_____
_____
_____
_____
_____
_____
_____
_____

OBSERVATION / *Write 3 - 4 observations*

_____
_____
_____
_____
_____
_____

APPLICATION / *Write down 1 - 2 applications*

PRAYER / *Write out a prayer over what you learned*

SOAP

Ephesians 6:12

For our struggle is not against flesh and blood,
but against the rulers, against the powers,
against the world rulers of this darkness, against
the spiritual forces of evil in the heavens.

INTO THE TEXT

We can guard ourselves against false friends, but we also need to remember who our real enemy is. There are people in our lives who will try to create dissension and division, but they are not the enemy—they are broken and sinful people just like us. The real battle is against the spiritual forces of evil in the world. God protects us and fights for us, but the ongoing spiritual battle continues to influence our lives. One of the ways it manifests itself is in our relationships.

The nation of Israel often had physical enemies to fight, but our struggle is not against people. Our battle is against the very real power of Satan. When we fight for peace and justice in our communities, we can easily make people out to be our ultimate enemy. This allows us to justify anything we need to do to defeat them, including sin. Instead, we should seek reconciliation and redemption for those who have wronged us, even while they face consequences for their actions.

PRAYER

God, help me remember who the real enemy is. Protect me, God, from the forces of evil still operating in the world. Give me opportunities to show love to the friends who have hurt me, and to show them Your redemptive love. Amen.

READ

Proverbs 22:24-25

Do not make friends with an angry person, and do not associate with a wrathful person, 25 lest you learn his ways and entangle yourself in a snare.

Proverbs 27:4

Wrath is cruel and anger is overwhelming, but who can stand before jealousy?

1 Corinthians 15:33

33 Do not be deceived: "Bad company corrupts good morals."

James 4:4-6

4 Adulterers, do you not know that friendship with the world means hostility toward God? So whoever decides to be the world's friend makes himself God's enemy. 5 Or do you think the scripture means nothing when it says, "The spirit that God caused to live within us has an envious yearning"? 6 But he gives greater grace. Therefore it says, "***God opposes the proud, but he gives grace to the humble.***"

SOAP / *James 4:4*
SCRIPTURE / *Write out the SOAP verses*

_____

_____

_____

_____

_____

_____

_____

_____

_____

_____

_____

_____

_____

_____

_____

_____

_____

_____

_____

_____

_____

_____

OBSERVATION / *Write 3 - 4 observations*

_____

_____

_____

_____

_____

_____

_____

APPLICATION / *Write down 1 - 2 applications*

PRAYER / *Write out a prayer over what you learned*

SOAP

James 4:4

Adulterers, do you not know that friendship with the world means hostility toward God? So whoever decides to be the world's friend makes himself God's enemy.

INTO THE TEXT

What does it mean to be friends with the world? Often in the New Testament, the world does not mean the literal earth that we live on (God said it was good when He made it!) but instead means something more along the lines of culture or human wisdom. God's creation is good, but the world now operates according to sin and death. Friendship with the world means that we have become too comfortable with the fallen order of things when we should be expectantly awaiting the redemption of this world.

In the case of friendship, the way of the world looks like anger, jealousy, and greed. That is the kind of worldly friendship that is incompatible with loving God. While we can certainly be friends with unbelievers, we also need to remember that we will be changed by the people we are closest to. We will pick up on their habits or be desensitized to the sin they justify. James' powerful words remind us to evaluate our closest relationships and ask, "Am I getting closer to the way of the world or am I getting closer to God?"

PRAYER

Lord, thank You for making me Your friend. Show me the places in my life where I am too comfortable with the way of the world and help me desire Your coming redemption. Amen.

READ

Ephesians 4:29

29 You must let no unwholesome word come out of your mouth, but only what is beneficial for the building up of the one in need, that it would give grace to those who hear.

Proverbs 16:24

Pleasant words are like a honeycomb, sweet to the soul and healing to the bones.

Proverbs 16:28

A perverse person spreads dissension, and a gossip separates the closest friends.

SOAP / *Ephesians 4:29*
SCRIPTURE / *Write out the SOAP verses*

_____

_____

_____

_____

_____

_____

_____

_____

_____

_____

_____

_____

_____

_____

_____

_____

_____

_____

_____

_____

_____

OBSERVATION / *Write 3 - 4 observations*

_____

_____

_____

_____

_____

_____

APPLICATION / *Write down 1 - 2 applications*

PRAYER / *Write out a prayer over what you learned*

SOAP

Ephesians 4:29

You must let no unwholesome word come out of your mouth, but only what is beneficial for the building up of the one in need, that it may give grace to those who hear.

INTO THE TEXT

Our words are more powerful than we can imagine. We use them carelessly, but they have the power to build up relationships or destroy them. Few of us can honestly say that every word that comes out of our mouths is beneficial, but this is the instruction given to the church in Ephesians. With a tool so powerful comes the responsibility to use it carefully. Rather than spouting off whatever comes to mind, whatever gets a laugh, or whatever feels good in the moment, we have the responsibility to ask: does this build up another person or tear them down?

Even words we think mean very little can have significant repercussions. A moment of harsh sarcasm or a joke that goes too far might be okay by the world's standards, but the bar is set higher for believers in this passage. When our words have the power to bring grace to those who need it, we should seriously reconsider using them for anything less than such a high calling.

PRAYER

God, help me understand the power of my words. Give me opportunities to use them to build other people up and convict me when I want to use them to tear other people down. Amen.

READ

1 Corinthians 13

If I speak in the tongues of men and of angels, but I do not have love, I am a noisy gong or a clanging cymbal. 2 And if I have prophecy, and know all mysteries and all knowledge, and if I have all faith so that I can remove mountains, but do not have love, I am nothing. 3 If I give away everything I own, and if I give over my body in order to boast, but do not have love, I receive no benefit. 4 Love is patient, love is kind, it is not envious. Love does not brag, it is not puffed up. 5 It is not rude, it is not self-serving, it is not easily angered or resentful. 6 It is not glad about injustice, but rejoices in the truth. 7 It bears all things, believes all things, hopes all things, endures all things. 8 Love never ends. But if there are prophecies, they will be set aside; if there are tongues, they will cease; if there is knowledge, it will be set aside. 9 For we know in part, and we prophesy in part, 10 but when what is perfect comes, the partial will be set aside. 11 When I was a child, I talked like a child, I thought like a child, I reasoned like a child. But when I became an adult, I set aside childish ways. 12 For now we see in a mirror indirectly, but then we will see face to face. Now I know in part, but then I will know fully, just as I have been fully known. 13 And now these three remain: faith, hope, and love. But the greatest of these is love.

Proverbs 12:26

The righteous person is cautious in his friendship, but the way of the wicked leads them astray.

SOAP / *1 Corinthians 13:4-7*
SCRIPTURE / *Write out the SOAP verses*

_____

_____

_____

_____

_____

_____

_____

_____

_____

_____

_____

_____

_____

_____

_____

_____

_____

_____

_____

_____

_____

OBSERVATION / *Write 3 - 4 observations*

_____

_____

_____

_____

_____

APPLICATION / *Write down 1 - 2 applications*

PRAYER / *Write out a prayer over what you learned*

SOAP

1 Corinthians 13:4-7

Love is patient, love is kind, it is not envious.
Love does not brag, it is not puffed up. It is not
rude, it is not self-serving, it is not easily angered
or resentful. It is not glad about injustice, but
rejoices in the truth. It bears all things, believes
all things, hopes all things, endures all things.

INTO THE TEXT

This passage from 1 Corinthians 13 is often used in weddings or on Valentine's Day cards, but these verses are not primarily for married couples. It was written in a letter to a church, in the context of teaching how the church functions as the body of Christ, using individuals' gifts for the sake of the whole community. We all need to be reminded that if we truly love our friends—and our church community should include some of our closest friends—then we will treat them the way true love does.

We can evaluate our friendships by looking at this long description and asking ourselves if our relationships look like this. Am I patient with my friends, am I kind to them, not envious of their possessions or talents? Do I brag or act arrogantly towards others? Am I rude? Do I have any other motivation for the friendship? Am I easily angered by their actions? Do I hold their sins against them? Am I honest with them? Do I bear their burdens, believe the best of their motivations, hope for the best things for them, and endure suffering and difficulty with them?

PRAYER

God, help me love my friends with this kind of love. Help me see where I need to grow and give me the grace that I need to do it. Amen.

1. *Are you a person who causes dissension? How can you ensure you are not a friend who creates obstacles and conflict in your relationships?*

....

....

....

2. *How does bad company corrupt good morals? How have you seen bad company impact your decisions and worldview?*

....

....

....

3. *Why does friendship with the world mean hostility toward God? What does friendship with the world look like? What can we do to guard against falling into friendship with the world?*

....

....

....

4. *Why are we instructed to watch what we say? How do your words impact your friendships? When have you hurt a friend with your words?*

....

....

....

5. *What does it mean that love rejoices with the truth? How can you live this out in your friendships?*

....

....

....

For the
Son of
Man
came to
seek and
to save
the lost.

Luke 19:10

*Write down your prayer requests
and praises for this week.*

....

....

....

....

....

....

....

....

....

....

....

....

WEEKLY CHALLENGE

*Jesus had different groups within His followers and friends: the large group of
disciples, the twelve apostles, and Peter, James, and John. How can we follow His
example of intimacy in friendship? How can you implement these principles in your
own life without being exclusive?*

....

....

....

....

....

....

....

READ

John 8:1-11

1 But Jesus went to the Mount of Olives. 2 Early in the morning he came to the temple courts again. All the people came to him, and he sat down and began to teach them. 3 The experts in the law and the Pharisees brought a woman who had been caught committing adultery. They made her stand in front of them 4 and said to Jesus, "Teacher, this woman was caught in the very act of adultery. 5 In the law *Moses commanded us to stone to death* such women. What then do you say?" 6 (Now they were asking this in an attempt to trap him, so that they could bring charges against him.) Jesus bent down and wrote on the ground with his finger. 7 When they persisted in asking him, he stood up straight and replied, "Whoever among you is guiltless may be the first to throw a stone at her." 8 Then he bent over again and wrote on the ground. 9 Now when they heard this, they began to drift away one at a time, starting with the older ones, until Jesus was left alone with the woman standing before him. 10 Jesus stood up straight and said to her, "Woman, where are they? Did no one condemn you?" 11 She replied, "No one, LORD." And Jesus said, "I do not condemn you either. Go, and from now on do not sin any more."

1 Timothy 1:15

15 This saying is trustworthy and deserves full acceptance: "Christ Jesus came into the world to save sinners"—and I am the worst of them!

Luke 5:31-32

31 Jesus answered them, "Those who are well don't need a physician, but those who are sick do. 32 I have not come to call the righteous, but sinners to repentance."

Luke 7:34-35

34 The Son of Man has come eating and drinking, and you say, 'Look at him, a glutton and a drunk, a friend of tax collectors and sinners!' 35 But wisdom is vindicated by all her children."

SOAP

SOAP / *1 Timothy 1:15*
SCRIPTURE / *Write out the SOAP verses*

_____

_____

_____

_____

_____

_____

_____

_____

_____

_____

_____

_____

_____

_____

_____

_____

_____

_____

_____

OBSERVATION / *Write 3 - 4 observations*

_____

_____

_____

_____

_____

_____

APPLICATION / *Write down 1 - 2 applications*

PRAYER / *Write out a prayer over what you learned*

SOAP

1 Timothy 1:15

This saying is trustworthy and deserves full acceptance: "Christ Jesus came into the world to save sinners"—and I am the worst of them!

INTO THE TEXT

The Gospels are filled with examples of Jesus getting in trouble for the kind of company He liked to keep. He defended sinful women, ate meals with tax collectors, and hung out with the poor, diseased, and marginalized. Jesus was a friend to people who hurt His reputation and did not deserve His friendship— people like us. He came to save sinners, and we are all certainly included in that group.

Paul's surprising statement to Timothy should remind us of our own posture—we are not better than the kind of people Jesus hung out with, we are exactly the same! When we accept Christ's free gift of grace, we have every reason to humble ourselves and admit that we are no better than the people we call sinners. There is no room for pride or self-righteousness when we honestly assess our situation. Christ became our friend when we did not deserve it, and our response should look like Paul's: a life poured out for the sake of others.

PRAYER

God, thank You for sending Your Son to be a friend to sinners like me. Thank You for seeking the lost and finding us. Help me to be that kind of friend to the marginalized around me. Amen.

READ

Mark 3:13-19

13 Now Jesus went up the mountain and called for those he wanted, and they came to him. 14 He appointed twelve so that they would be with him and he could send them to preach 15 and to have authority to cast out demons. 16 To Simon he gave the name Peter; 17 to James and his brother John, the sons of Zebedee, he gave the name Boanerges (that is, "sons of thunder"); 18 and Andrew, Philip, Bartholomew, Matthew, Thomas, James the son of Alphaeus, Thaddaeus, Simon the Zealot, 19 and Judas Iscariot, who betrayed him.

Mark 5:37

37 He did not let anyone follow him except Peter, James, and John, the brother of James.

Mark 9:2-8

2 Six days later Jesus took with him Peter, James, and John and led them alone up a high mountain privately. And he was transfigured before them, 3 and his clothes became radiantly white, more so than any launderer in the world could bleach them. 4 Then Elijah appeared before them along with Moses, and they were talking with Jesus. 5 So Peter said to Jesus, "Rabbi, it is good for us to be here. Let us make three shelters—one for you, one for Moses, and one for Elijah." 6 (For they were afraid, and he did not know what to say.) 7 Then a cloud overshadowed them, and a voice came from the cloud, "This is my one dear Son. Listen to him!" 8 Suddenly when they looked around, they saw no one with them any more except Jesus.

SOAP / *Mark 9:2*
SCRIPTURE / *Write out the SOAP verses*

_____

OBSERVATION / *Write 3 - 4 observations*

APPLICATION / *Write down 1 - 2 applications*

_____

_____

_____

_____

_____

_____

_____

_____

_____

_____

_____

_____

_____

PRAYER / *Write out a prayer over what you learned*

_____

_____

_____

_____

_____

_____

_____

_____

_____

_____

_____

_____

_____

_____

_____

_____

SOAP

Mark 9:2

Six days later Jesus took with him Peter, James, and John and led them alone up a high mountain privately. And he was transfigured before them

INTO THE TEXT

Even Jesus needed a few close friends. The scene of the transfiguration in Mark 9 is a stunning account of Jesus revealing to a few of His disciples a glimpse of His coming kingdom and glory. While Jesus selected a few disciples as those closest to Him, there is another set of friends in this story worth noting. After Jesus is transfigured, Moses and Elijah appeared with Him. Moses represented the law and Elijah represented the prophets, the revelation of God in the Old Testament. However, the law and the prophets were only shadows. The law and prophets were revelations from God, but Jesus is the ultimate revelation of God.

Mark 9:4 says that Moses and Elijah were talking with Jesus—what were they talking about? Luke's account (9:28-36) tells us that they were discussing His departure at Jerusalem. In this crucial moment before His death and resurrection, Jesus spoke with some friends who knew a little more than His disciples did. None of us have experienced anything close to what Jesus discussed with Moses and Elijah, but this astonishing story makes clear that Jesus Himself needed friends who could bear His burdens with Him, knowing the suffering He was about to endure.

PRAYER

God, thank You for the Incarnation. Thank You for Your Son who has intimately experienced what it means to be human and who shows us our need for human friendship. Show me how to build those kinds of relationships in my life. Amen.

WEEK 5

Wednesday

READ

Luke 15:1-10

Now all the tax collectors and sinners were coming to hear him. 2 But the Pharisees and the experts in the law were complaining, "This man welcomes sinners and eats with them." 3 So Jesus told them this parable: 4 "Which one of you, if he has a hundred sheep and loses one of them, would not leave the ninety-nine in the open pasture and go look for the one that is lost until he finds it? 5 Then when he has found it, he places it on his shoulders, rejoicing. 6 Returning home, he calls together his friends and neighbors, telling them, 'Rejoice with me, because I have found my sheep that was lost.' 7 I tell you, in the same way there will be more joy in heaven over one sinner who repents than over ninety-nine righteous people who have no need to repent. 8 "Or what woman, if she has ten silver coins and loses one of them, does not light a lamp, sweep the house, and search thoroughly until she finds it? 9 Then when she has found it, she calls together her friends and neighbors, saying, 'Rejoice with me, for I have found the coin that I had lost.' 10 In the same way, I tell you, there is joy in the presence of God's angels over one sinner who repents."

Luke 19:1-10

Jesus entered Jericho and was passing through it. 2 Now a man named Zacchaeus was there; he was a chief tax collector and was rich. 3 He was trying to get a look at Jesus, but being a short man he could not see over the crowd. 4 So he ran on ahead and climbed up into a sycamore tree to see him, because Jesus was going to pass that way. 5 And when Jesus came to that place, he looked up and said to him, "Zacchaeus, come down quickly, because I must stay at your house today." 6 So he came down quickly and welcomed Jesus joyfully. 7 And when the people saw it, they all complained, "He has gone in to be the guest of a man who is a sinner." 8 But Zacchaeus stopped and said to the LORD, "Look, LORD, half of my possessions I now give to the poor, and if I have cheated anyone of anything, I am paying back four times as much!" 9 Then Jesus said to him, "Today salvation has come to this household, because he too is a son of Abraham! 10 For the Son of Man came to seek and to save the lost."

SOAP / *Luke 19:10*
SCRIPTURE / *Write out the SOAP verses*

_____

_____

_____

_____

_____

_____

_____

_____

_____

_____

_____

_____

_____

_____

_____

_____

_____

_____

_____

_____

_____

_____

_____

OBSERVATION / *Write 3 - 4 observations*

_____

_____

_____

_____

_____

_____

_____

APPLICATION / *Write down 1 - 2 applications*

_____

_____

_____

_____

_____

_____

_____

_____

_____

_____

_____

_____

PRAYER / *Write out a prayer over what you learned*

_____

_____

_____

_____

_____

_____

_____

_____

_____

_____

_____

_____

_____

_____

_____

SOAP

Luke 19:10

For the Son of Man came to seek and to save the lost.

INTO THE TEXT

When we hear such a succinct statement of Jesus' ministry it can be tempting to boil down His message. We can simplify it to a spiritual message stripped of everything earthy and material. But the title of Son of Man encapsulates Jesus' whole earthly ministry. Luke presents Jesus as the Savior of all humanity, the new Adam, the originator of a new people. He has come not just to seek out the one lost sheep or coin, but to incorporate the lost into His new family, new nation, new people: the redeemed.

This illustrates how our vertical and horizontal relationships are so intimately connected. When we are redeemed, we are not only reconciled to God, but we are also incorporated into the new creation He has already begun. Luke's entire Gospel illustrates this: when Jesus began His ministry, He announced that He was coming to uplift the poor, release the captives, give sight to the blind, set the oppressed free, and proclaim the year of the Lord's favor (4:18). He came to inaugurate the new creation that will one day be consummated. He came to seek and save us, the lost, as part of His entire redemptive project.

PRAYER

God, thank You for seeking and saving me! Thank You for the new creation that is coming. Help me live in light of that reality as a member of Your family. Amen.

READ

Mark 12:30-31

Love the LORD your God with all your heart, with all your soul, with all your mind, and with all your strength.' 31 The second is: '**Love your neighbor as yourself.**' There is no other commandment greater than these."

Galatians 5:14-17

14 For the whole law can be summed up in a single commandment, namely, "**You must love your neighbor as yourself.**" 15 However, if you continually bite and devour one another, beware that you are not consumed by one another. 16 But I say, live by the Spirit and you will not carry out the desires of the flesh. 17 For the flesh has desires that are opposed to the Spirit, and the Spirit has desires that are opposed to the flesh, for these are in opposition to each other, so that you cannot do what you want.

SOAP

WEEK 5 · THURSDAY

SOAP / *Galatians 5:14*
SCRIPTURE / *Write out the SOAP verses*

_____

_____

_____

_____

_____

_____

_____

_____

_____

_____

_____

_____

_____

_____

_____

_____

_____

_____

_____

_____

_____

_____

OBSERVATION / *Write 3 - 4 observations*

_____

_____

_____

_____

_____

_____

APPLICATION / *Write down 1 - 2 applications*

PRAYER / *Write out a prayer over what you learned*

SOAP

Galatians 5:14

For the whole law can be summed up in a single commandment, namely, "**You must love your neighbor as yourself.** "

INTO THE TEXT

There are a lot of laws in the Old Testament, and they paint a picture for us of how God's people were supposed to live. Some of them seem strange or unnecessary to us, but they provided boundaries for God's people, showing them how to live in community in a way that glorified Him. All those laws that outlined specifically how this community should work and live can be summed up in this one important law: love your neighbor as yourself.

This is how our love for God is evidenced: by loving the most vulnerable and unlovable among us, just as He did. When Jesus referenced this law in the story of the Good Samaritan (Lk 10:25-37), He intended to show the expert in the law that his thinking was too small. You should not try to limit the definition of your neighbor; you should willingly expand it to include whoever God puts in your path. The same is true for us: rather than quibble over what obligations we have to which people, we can freely offer our love and service to the more vulnerable around us.

PRAYER

God, show me how to love like You did. Show me who my neighbor is, and how I can serve them. Thank You for loving me when I do not deserve it. Amen.

READ

Acts 2:42-47

42 They were devoting themselves to the apostles' teaching and to fellowship, to the breaking of bread and to prayer. 43 Reverential awe came over everyone, and many wonders and miraculous signs came about by the apostles. 44 All who believed were together and held everything in common, 45 and they began selling their property and possessions and distributing the proceeds to everyone, as anyone had need. 46 Every day they continued to gather together by common consent in the temple courts, breaking bread from house to house, sharing their food with glad and humble hearts, 47 praising God and having the good will of all the people. And the LORD was adding to their number every day those who were being saved.

Acts 20:7

7 On the first day of the week, when we met to break bread, Paul began to speak to the people, and because he intended to leave the next day, he extended his message until midnight.

SOAP / *Acts 2:46-47*
SCRIPTURE / *Write out the SOAP verses*

_____

_____

_____

_____

_____

_____

_____

_____

_____

_____

_____

_____

_____

_____

_____

_____

_____

_____

_____

_____

OBSERVATION / *Write 3 - 4 observations*

_____

_____

_____

_____

_____

_____

APPLICATION / *Write down 1 - 2 applications*

PRAYER / *Write out a prayer over what you learned*

SOAP

Acts 2:46-47

Every day they continued to gather together by common consent in the temple courts, breaking bread from house to house, sharing their food with glad and humble hearts, praising God and having the good will of all the people. And the LORD was adding to their number every day those who were being saved.

INTO THE TEXT

In a world with sermons and worship music easily accessible online, many people wonder what the value even is for a brick-and-mortar church. If the point of our meeting is merely to learn more about the Bible, then there is no reason for us to meet in person. Yet this account of the early church reminds us that there is something more significant about meeting together. When we spend time together, eating and drinking, talking and laughing, sharing our stories and building community, we are witnessing to the goodness of the coming kingdom of God. There is nothing that can replace it.

God works through our meetings—He drew people to Himself through these early church meetings and He continues to use the witness of our relationships with one another to draw people to Himself. People can download a sermon podcast or listen to worship music from the comfort of their home, but there is no replacement for flesh and blood community.

PRAYER

Lord, thank You for the gift of fellowship with believers! Help me cultivate good relationships in my church community that witness to You and draw people closer to knowing You. Amen.

1. *What was Jesus' attitude when He interacted with sinners? How did He love them and encourage them to leave their life of sin?*

....

....

....

2. *What was Jesus' purpose in coming to earth? How did He display His purposes through His actions with those considered 'sinners'?*

....

....

....

3. *What does it mean to love your neighbor as yourself? (Hint: it is not about loving yourself first!)*

....

....

....

4. *What things did the early church do to foster community?*

....

....

....

5. *Why is sharing a meal a significant community experience? What does a shared meal communicate to those involved?*

....

....

....

No one has greater love than this—that one lays down his life for his friends.

John 15:13

PRAY

*Write down your prayer requests
and praises for this week.*

....

....

....

....

....

....

....

....

....

....

....

....

....

WEEKLY CHALLENGE

*Paul commanded the Romans to show eagerness in honoring one another (Rom 12:10).
This week, go out of your way to honor three friends. Do so in such a way that it does
not bring you any recognition, but only honors and encourages your friends.*

....

....

....

....

....

....

....

....

READ

1 Peter 5:6-7

6 And God will exalt you in due time, if you humble yourselves under his mighty hand 7 by casting all your cares on him because he cares for you.

SOAP / *1 Peter 5:7*
SCRIPTURE / *Write out the SOAP verses*

_____

_____

_____

_____

_____

_____

_____

_____

_____

_____

_____

_____

_____

_____

_____

_____

_____

_____

_____

_____

_____

_____

OBSERVATION / *Write 3 - 4 observations*

_____

_____

_____

_____

_____

_____

APPLICATION / *Write down 1 - 2 applications*

PRAYER / *Write out a prayer over what you learned*

SOAP

1 Peter 5:7

by casting all your cares on him because he cares for you.

INTO THE TEXT

We were made for human relationships, but a fallen world means that many of our relationships will disappoint us or even hurt us. Ultimately, our needs are met by God, never by humans. When we face loneliness, fear, and pain, we can rely on God to bear our burdens and offer comfort. When our friends are not reliable, God always is.

God does not promise to alleviate our pain, heal our sickness, or end our suffering on earth. But our ultimate hope is in total restoration in eternity. We can cast our cares on God knowing that He cares for us because He demonstrated this love by sending His Son to die on the cross for us. Our friends may fail us, but God never will. Our friends may prioritize their own desires over our well-being, but Christ suffered and died for our sake. Our friends may shrug off our burdens, but God promises to trade our heavy weights for an easy yoke (Mt 11:30).

PRAYER

Thank You, God, that You never fail me! I pray that You will give me friendships that honor You and bring me joy. I thank You that You remain my ultimate source of comfort and security. Amen.

READ

John 15:14-17

14 You are my friends if you do what I command you. 15 I no longer call you slaves, because the slave does not understand what his master is doing. But I have called you friends, because I have revealed to you everything I heard from my Father. 16 You did not choose me, but I chose you and appointed you to go and bear fruit, fruit that remains, so that whatever you ask the Father in my name he will give you. 17 This I command you—to love one another.

SOAP / *John 15:15*
SCRIPTURE / *Write out the SOAP verses*

OBSERVATION / *Write 3 - 4 observations*

APPLICATION / *Write down 1 - 2 applications*

PRAYER / *Write out a prayer over what you learned*

SOAP

John 15:15

I no longer call you slaves, because the slave does not understand what his master is doing. But I have called you friends, because I have revealed to you everything I heard from my Father.

INTO THE TEXT

We are not worthy to be called friends of God, but by His grace, we receive the honor of that relationship. Israel's identity was built on remembering what God had done for them by bringing them out of bondage in Egypt. They had been liberated, and their response was worship. They already knew God as the one who freed people from slavery, but they still understood the appropriate distance one keeps from a holy God. They also knew God's law, but not always the reason behind it. When Jesus said that He no longer called His disciples slaves but, instead, friends, He explained one significant implication of the Incarnation: God revealing Himself to us.

We still know God only in part, and we will spend all eternity learning more. When Jesus entered the world, He chose to reveal the character of God in an intimate and direct way. In this moment with the disciples, He revealed even more to them, and this knowledge changed the relationship. We are called friends of God because of the glimpse we have been given into His grand redemptive plan.

PRAYER

God, thank You for revealing Yourself to me! Thank You for the incarnation, and the relationship this revelation allowed between us. Help me show the world this relationship I have with You. Amen.

READ

Proverbs 18:24

There are companions who harm one another, but there is a friend who sticks closer than a brother.

Hebrews 13:5-6

5 Your conduct must be free from the love of money and you must be content with what you have, for he has said, "*I will never leave you and I will never abandon you.*" 6 So we can say with confidence, "*The Lord is my helper, and I will not be afraid. What can people do to me?*"

SOAP / *Proverbs 18:24*
SCRIPTURE / *Write out the SOAP verses*

OBSERVATION / *Write 3 - 4 observations*

APPLICATION / *Write down 1 - 2 applications*

_____

_____

_____

_____

_____

_____

_____

_____

_____

_____

_____

_____

_____

PRAYER / *Write out a prayer over what you learned*

_____

_____

_____

_____

_____

_____

_____

_____

_____

_____

_____

_____

_____

_____

_____

_____

SOAP

Proverbs 18:24

*There are companions who harm one another, but there
is a friend who sticks closer than a brother.*

INTO THE TEXT

Some of us have not only been disappointed by our
friends, we have been seriously hurt. Close relationships
are a gift of God, but with closeness comes certain
risks. The people closest to us can hurt us in especially
painful ways, even abusing or taking advantage of us.
We may have experienced other friendships that were
healthy and positive, but even one seriously harmful
relationship can make it difficult to maintain others.

When our understanding of relationships has been
marred by abuse, we can think God works the same way.
Our God offers hope and comfort to us when we have
been abused or abandoned. We are promised that God
is faithful to us in ways that no friend or family member
can ever be. He never changes, He never fails, and His
promises are always fulfilled. We have been given the
gift of Scripture to remind us of His faithfulness. Over
and over again He sees us, loves us, and refuses to give
up on His children.

PRAYER

Thank You, God, that You are faithful and good! Bring
me comfort, God, when I am hurt by others. Help me
trust You despite the evil around me and bring me peace
that can only come from You. Amen.

READ

John 15:13

13 No one has greater love than this—that one lays down his life for his friends.

Romans 5:8

8 But God demonstrates his own love for us, in that while we were still sinners, Christ died for us.

Ephesians 5:1-2

Therefore, be imitators of God as dearly loved children 2 and live in love, just as Christ also loved us and gave himself for us, a sacrificial and fragrant offering to God.

SOAP / *John 15:13*
SCRIPTURE / *Write out the SOAP verses*

_____
_____
_____
_____
_____
_____
_____
_____
_____
_____
_____
_____
_____
_____
_____
_____
_____
_____
_____

OBSERVATION / *Write 3 - 4 observations*

_____
_____
_____
_____
_____
_____

APPLICATION / *Write down 1 - 2 applications*

PRAYER / *Write out a prayer over what you learned*

SOAP

John 15:13

*No one has greater love than this—that
one lays down his life for his friends.*

INTO THE TEXT

Jesus displayed the greatest love for us by laying down
His life for our sake. Not only does He make this
ultimate sacrifice on behalf of His friends, but He
does also it for His enemies. He died for the ones who
shouted for His crucifixion, the ones who opposed His
ministry, even the disciples who would abandon Him
on the cross. He died for us as well—people who sin
against Him, hurt His children, and often misrepresent
Him to the world. He showed the ultimate love in
dying for those He called friends even when they were
acting like enemies.

We are called to imitate such selfless love in our own
communities. Just as Christ demonstrated His love by
His actions, we are called to demonstrate our love to
the world by our actions. We can follow His example
by seeking out those the world ignores and showing
them compassion. We can witness to the truth of
Christ's sacrifice by showing the world that we are also
willing to sacrifice our preferences and comfort for the
sake of another.

PRAYER

God, thank You for making the ultimate sacrifice for
me. Thank You for loving me like a friend even when I
was Your enemy. Give me the grace to show that kind
of love to others. Amen.

READ

Philippians 2:1-18

Therefore, if there is any encouragement in Christ, any comfort provided by love, any fellowship in the Spirit, any affection or mercy, 2 complete my joy and be of the same mind, by having the same love, being united in spirit, and having one purpose. 3 Instead of being motivated by selfish ambition or vanity, each of you should, in humility, be moved to treat one another as more important than yourself. 4 Each of you should be concerned not only about your own interests, but about the interests of others as well. 5 You should have the same attitude toward one another that Christ Jesus had, 6 who though he existed in the form of God did not regard equality with God as something to be grasped, 7 but emptied himself by taking on the form of a slave, by looking like other men, and by sharing in human nature. 8 He humbled himself, by becoming obedient to the point of death —even death on a cross! 9 As a result God highly exalted him and gave him the name that is above every name, 10 so that at the name of Jesus every knee will bow —in heaven and on earth and under the earth— 11 and every tongue confess that Jesus Christ is LORD to the glory of God the Father. 12 So then, my dear friends, just as you have always obeyed, not only in my presence but even more in my absence, continue working out your salvation with awe and reverence, 13 for the one bringing forth in you both the desire and the effort—for the sake of his good pleasure—is God. 14 Do everything without grumbling or arguing, 15 so that you may be blameless and pure, children of God without blemish though you live in a crooked and perverse society, in which you shine as lights in the world 16 by holding on to the word of life so that on the day of Christ I will have a reason to boast that I did not run in vain nor labor in vain. 17 But even if I am being poured out like a drink offering on the sacrifice and service of your faith, I am glad and rejoice together with all of you. 18 And in the same way you also should be glad and rejoice together with me.

Romans 12:9-21

9 Love must be without hypocrisy. Abhor what is evil, cling to what is good. 10 Be devoted to one another with mutual love, showing eagerness in honoring one another. 11 Do not lag in zeal, be enthusiastic in spirit, serve the LORD. 12 Rejoice in hope, endure in suffering, persist in prayer. 13 Contribute to the needs of the saints, pursue hospitality. 14 Bless those who persecute you, bless and do not curse. 15 Rejoice with those who rejoice, weep with those who weep. 16 Live in harmony with one another; do not be haughty but associate with the lowly. Do not be conceited. 17 Do not repay anyone evil for evil; consider what is good before all people. 18 If possible, so far as it depends on you, live peaceably with all people. 19 Do not avenge yourselves, dear friends, but give place to God's wrath, for it is written, "***Vengeance is mine, I will repay,***" says the LORD. 20 Rather, ***if your enemy is hungry, feed him; if he is thirsty, give him a drink; for in doing this you will be heaping burning coals on his head***. 21 Do not be overcome by evil, but overcome evil with good.

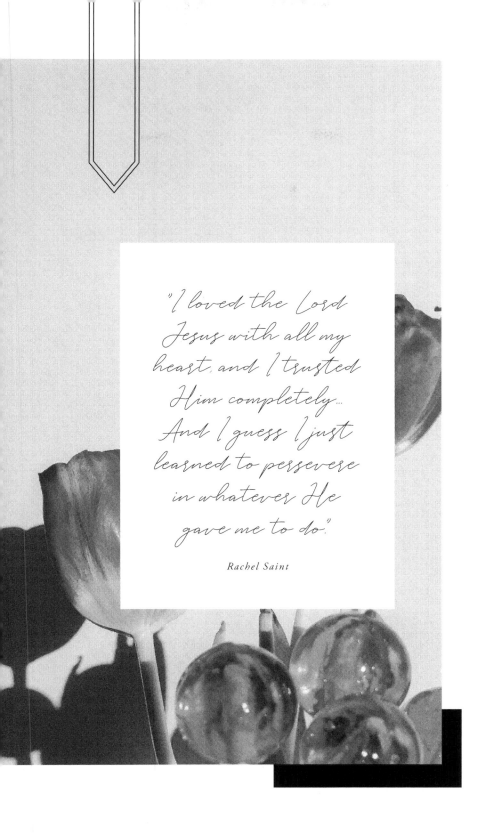

"I loved the Lord Jesus with all my heart, and I trusted Him completely... And I guess I just learned to persevere in whatever He gave me to do."

Rachel Saint

SOAP

SOAP / *Romans 12:9-10*
SCRIPTURE / *Write out the SOAP verses*

_____

_____

_____

_____

_____

_____

_____

_____

_____

_____

_____

_____

_____

_____

_____

_____

_____

_____

_____

_____

OBSERVATION / *Write 3 - 4 observations*

_____

_____

_____

_____

_____

_____

_____

APPLICATION / *Write down 1 - 2 applications*

PRAYER / *Write out a prayer over what you learned*

SOAP

Romans 12:9-10
Love must be without hypocrisy. Abhor what is evil,
cling to what is good. Be devoted to one another with
mutual love, showing eagerness in honoring one another.

INTO THE TEXT

This is perhaps Scripture's most fundamental teaching on human relationships: prioritize others above yourself. This is what "showing eagerness in honoring one another" means, that we are to outdo each another in honoring one another. We are called to humble ourselves, submitting our preferences and desires to the good of our community. In a healthy community, however, our needs are not forgotten, because others are showing eagerness in honoring us. There is mutual love, each of us seeking the good of the others.

If this sounds unrealistic and impractical, that's because it is. God has graciously given us instructions in Scripture about how to structure our communities and cultivate good relationships, but none of those instructions can be done without His grace and none will be followed perfectly until eternity. Our hope is not in our own efforts to do good and love one another. Our hope is in God's love for us—a love that motivates our love for each other, equips us to love each other, and gives us hope for a sinless future in which our relationships will be redeemed.

PRAYER

Thank You, God, that You love us perfectly. Give us the grace we need to love each other well and honor the needs of our whole community. Thank You for the gift of friendships. Amen.

1. What does it mean to cast your cares on Jesus? How can you do this on a daily basis?

....

....

....

2. How does following Jesus' commands make us His friends?

....

....

....

3. When in your life have you seen God provide you with friends when you needed them most? How does His provision give you encouragement that He will continue to do this in the future?

....

....

....

4. Jesus laid down His life for His friends. How did this action display His great love for us? What does this show us about how He views us?

....

....

....

5. What does it mean to have love without hypocrisy? How can we be devoted to one another with mutual love?

....

....

....

Have you developed a consistent, daily Bible study habit
and don't want to break it before our next study begins?
In the following pages, you can continue your quiet
time with our suggested reading and SOAP passages.

WEEK 1

○ *Monday*
Reading: Psalm 81-82
SOAP: Psalm 81:10

○ *Tuesday:*
Reading: Psalm 83-84
SOAP: Psalm 84:11-12

○ *Wednesday*
Reading: Psalm 85-86
SOAP: Psalm 86:17

○ *Thursday*
Reading: Psalm 87-88
SOAP: Psalm 88:13-14

○ *Friday*
Reading: Psalm 89-90
SOAP: Psalm 89:32

WEEK 2

○ *Monday*
Reading: Psalm 91-92
SOAP: Psalm 91:15

○ *Tuesday*
Reading: Psalm 93-94
SOAP: Psalm 94:12-13

○ *Wednesday*
Reading: Psalm 95-96
SOAP: Psalm 96:1-3

○ *Thursday*
Reading: Psalm 97-98
SOAP: Psalm 96:1-3

○ *Friday*
Reading: Psalm 99-100
SOAP: Psalm 100:5

For the Lord God
is our sovereign
protector. The
Lord bestows
favor and honor;
he withholds
no good thing
from those who
have integrity.
O Lord of
Heaven's Armies,
how blessed
are those who
trust in you.

Psalm 84:11-12

PRAY

Write down your prayer requests
and praises for this week.

Psalm 81

*For the music director, according to
the* gittith *style; by Asaph.*

1 Shout for joy to God, our source of strength!
Shout out to the God of Jacob!
2 Sing a song and play the tambourine,
the pleasant-sounding harp, and the
ten-stringed instrument.
3 Sound the ram's horn on the day of the new moon,
and on the day of the full moon when our festival begins.
4 For observing the festival is a requirement for Israel;
it is an ordinance given by the God of Jacob.
5 He decreed it as a regulation in Joseph,
when he attacked the land of Egypt.
I heard a voice I did not recognize.
6 It said: "I removed the burden from his shoulder;
his hands were released from holding the basket.
7 In your distress you called out and I rescued you.
I answered you from a dark thundercloud.
I tested you at the waters of Meribah. (Selah)
8 I said, 'Listen, my people!
I will warn you.
O Israel, if only you would obey me!
9 There must be no other god among you.
You must not worship a foreign god.
10 I am the Lord, your God,
the one who brought you out of the land of Egypt.
Open your mouth wide and I will fill it.'
11 But my people did not obey me;
Israel did not submit to me.
12 I gave them over to their stubborn desires;
they did what seemed right to them.
13 If only my people would obey me!
If only Israel would keep my commands!
14 Then I would quickly subdue their enemies,
and attack their adversaries."
15 (May those who hate the Lord

Psalm 81 (Continued)

cower in fear before him.
May they be permanently humiliated.)
16 "I would feed Israel the best wheat,
and would satisfy your appetite with
honey from the rocky cliffs."

Psalm 82

A psalm of Asaph.

1 God stands in the assembly of El;
in the midst of the gods he renders judgment.
2 He says, "How long will you
make unjust legal decisions
and show favoritism to the wicked? (Selah)
3 Defend the cause of the poor and the fatherless.
Vindicate the oppressed and suffering.
4 Rescue the poor and needy.
Deliver them from the power of the wicked.
5 They neither know nor understand.
They stumble around in the dark,
while all the foundations of the earth crumble.
6 I thought, 'You are gods;
all of you are sons of the Most High.'
7 Yet you will die like mortals;
you will fall like all the other rulers."
8 Rise up, O God, and execute judgment on the earth!
For you own all the nations.

JOURNAL

your thoughts

....
....
....
....
....
....
....
....
....
....
....
....
....
....
....
....
....
....

SOAP

SOAP / *Psalm 81:10*
SCRIPTURE / *Write out the SOAP verses*

_____

_____

_____

_____

_____

_____

_____

_____

_____

_____

_____

_____

_____

_____

_____

_____

_____

_____

_____

_____

_____

_____

OBSERVATION / *Write 3 - 4 observations*

_____

_____

_____

_____

_____

_____

_____

APPLICATION / *Write down 1 - 2 applications*

PRAYER / *Write out a prayer over what you learned*

THANKFUL

WEEK 1 • MONDAY

*Write three things you are thankful for
today and why each one brings you joy.*

ONE

....
....
....
....
....
....
....

TWO

....
....
....
....
....
....
....

THREE

....
....
....
....
....
....
....

Psalm 83

A song, a psalm of Asaph.

1 O God, do not be silent.
Do not ignore us. Do not be inactive, O God.
2 For look, your enemies are making a commotion;
those who hate you are hostile.
3 They carefully plot against your people,
and make plans to harm the ones you cherish.
4 They say, "Come on, let's annihilate
them so they are no longer a nation.
Then the name of Israel will be remembered no more."
5 Yes, they devise a unified strategy;
they form an alliance against you.
6 It includes the tents of Edom and the Ishmaelites,
Moab and the Hagrites,
7 Gebal, Ammon, and Amalek,
Philistia and the inhabitants of Tyre.
8 Even Assyria has allied with them,
lending its strength to the descendants of Lot. (Selah)
9 Do to them as you did to Midian—
as you did to Sisera and Jabin at the Kishon River.
10 They were destroyed at Endor;
their corpses were like manure on the ground.
11 Make their nobles like Oreb and Zeeb,
and all their rulers like Zebah and Zalmunna,
12 who said, "Let's take over the pastures of God."
13 O my God, make them like dead thistles,
like dead weeds blown away by the wind.
14 Like the fire that burns down the forest,
or the flames that consume the mountainsides,
15 chase them with your gale winds,
and terrify them with your windstorm.
16 Cover their faces with shame,
so they might seek you, O LORD.
17 May they be humiliated and continually terrified.
May they die in shame.
18 Then they will know that you alone are the LORD,
the Most High over all the earth.

Psalm 84

For the music director, according to the gittith
style; written by the Korahites, a psalm.

1 How lovely is the place where you live,
O Lord of Heaven's Armies!
2 I desperately want to be
in the courts of the Lord's temple.
My heart and my entire being shout for joy
to the living God.
3 Even the birds find a home there,
and the swallow builds a nest,
where she can protect her young
near your altars, O Lord of Heaven's Armies,
my King and my God.
4 How blessed are those who live in your temple
and praise you continually. (Selah)
5 How blessed are those who find their strength in you,
and long to travel the roads that lead to your temple.
6 As they pass through the Baca Valley,
he provides a spring for them.
The rain even covers it with pools of water.
7 They are sustained as they travel along;
each one appears before God in Zion.
8 O Lord God of Heaven's Armies,
hear my prayer.
Listen, O God of Jacob. (Selah)
9 O God, take notice of our shield.
Show concern for your chosen king.
10 Certainly spending just one day in
your temple courts is better
than spending a thousand elsewhere.
I would rather stand at the entrance
to the temple of my God
than live in the tents of the wicked.
11 For the Lord God is our sovereign protector.
The Lord bestows favor and honor;
he withholds no good thing from those who have integrity.
12 O Lord of Heaven's Armies,
how blessed are those who trust in you.

"The eagle
that soars in
the upper air
does not worry
itself how it is
to cross rivers."

Gladys Aylward

SOAP / *Psalm 84:11-12*
SCRIPTURE / *Write out the SOAP verses*

OBSERVATION / *Write 3 - 4 observations*

APPLICATION / *Write down 1 - 2 applications*

PRAYER / *Write out a prayer over what you learned*

THANKFUL

WEEK 1 • TUESDAY

*Write three things you are thankful for
today and why each one brings you joy.*

ONE

....
....
....
....
....
....
....

TWO

....
....
....
....
....
....
....

THREE

....
....
....
....
....
....
....

Psalm 85

*For the music director, written by
the Korahites, a psalm.*

1 O Lord, you showed favor to your land;
you restored the well-being of Jacob.
2 You pardoned the wrongdoing of your people;
you forgave all their sin. (Selah)
3 You withdrew all your fury;
you turned back from your raging anger.
4 Restore us, O God our deliverer.
Do not be displeased with us.
5 Will you stay mad at us forever?
Will you remain angry throughout future generations?
6 Will you not revive us once more?
Then your people will rejoice in you.
7 O Lord, show us your loyal love.
Bestow on us your deliverance.
8 I will listen to what God the Lord says.
For he will make peace with his
people, his faithful followers.
Yet they must not return to their foolish ways.
9 Certainly his loyal followers will
soon experience his deliverance;
then his splendor will again appear in our land.
10 Loyal love and faithfulness meet;
deliverance and peace greet each other with a kiss.
11 Faithfulness grows from the ground,
and deliverance looks down from the sky.
12 Yes, the Lord will bestow his good blessings,
and our land will yield its crops.
13 Deliverance goes before him,
and prepares a pathway for him.

Psalm 86

A prayer of David.

1 Listen, O Lord. Answer me.
For I am oppressed and needy.
2 Protect me, for I am loyal.
You are my God; deliver your servant who trusts in you.
3 Have mercy on me, O Lord,
for I cry out to you all day long.
4 Make your servant glad,
for to you, O Lord, I pray.
5 Certainly, O Lord, you are kind and forgiving,
and show great faithfulness to all who cry out to you.
6 O Lord, hear my prayer.
Pay attention to my plea for mercy.
7 In my time of trouble I cry out to you,
for you will answer me.
8 None can compare to you among the gods, O Lord.
Your exploits are incomparable.
9 All the nations, whom you created,
will come and worship you, O Lord.
They will honor your name.
10 For you are great and do amazing things.
You alone are God.
11 O Lord, teach me how you want me to live.
Then I will obey your commands.
Make me wholeheartedly committed to you.
12 O Lord, my God, I will give you
thanks with my whole heart.
I will honor your name continually.
13 For you will extend your great loyal love to me,
and will deliver my life from the depths of Sheol.
14 O God, arrogant men attack me;
a gang of ruthless men, who do not
respect you, seek my life.

Psalm 86 (Continued)

15 But you, O LORD, are a
compassionate and merciful God.
You are patient and demonstrate great
loyal love and faithfulness.
16 Turn toward me and have mercy on me.
Give your servant your strength.
Deliver this son of your female servant.
17 Show me evidence of your favor.
Then those who hate me will see it and be ashamed,
for you, O LORD, will help me and comfort me.

SOAP

SOAP / *Psalm 86:17*
SCRIPTURE / *Write out the SOAP verses*

_____

_____

_____

_____

_____

_____

_____

_____

_____

_____

_____

_____

_____

_____

_____

_____

_____

_____

_____

_____

OBSERVATION / *Write 3 - 4 observations*

_____

_____

_____

_____

_____

_____

APPLICATION / *Write down 1 - 2 applications*

PRAYER / *Write out a prayer over what you learned*

THANKFUL

*Write three things you are thankful for
today and why each one brings you joy.*

ONE

....
....
....
....
....
....
....

TWO

....
....
....
....
....
....
....

THREE

....
....
....
....
....
....
....

Psalm 87

Written by the Korahites; a psalm, a song.

1 The Lord's city is in the holy hills.
2 The Lord loves the gates of Zion
more than all the dwelling places of Jacob.
3 People say wonderful things about you,
O city of God. (Selah)
4 I mention Rahab and Babylon to my followers.
Here are Philistia and Tyre, along with Ethiopia.
It is said of them, "This one was born there."
5 But it is said of Zion's residents,
"Each one of these was born in her,
and the Most High makes her secure."
6 The Lord writes in the census book of the nations,
"This one was born there." (Selah)
7 As for the singers, as well as the pipers—
all of them sing within your walls.

Psalm 88

A song, a psalm written by the Korahites, for the
music director, according to the machalath-leannoth
style; a well-written song by Heman the Ezrahite.

1 O Lord God who delivers me,
by day I cry out
and at night I pray before you.
2 Listen to my prayer.
Pay attention to my cry for help.
3 For my life is filled with troubles,
and I am ready to enter Sheol.
4 They treat me like those who descend into the grave.
I am like a helpless man,
5 adrift among the dead,
like corpses lying in the grave,
whom you remember no more,
and who are cut off from your power.

Psalm 88 (Continued)

6 You place me in the lowest regions of the Pit,
in the dark places, in the watery depths.
7 Your anger bears down on me,
and you overwhelm me with all your waves. (Selah)
8 You cause those who know me to keep their distance;
you make me an appalling sight to them.
I am trapped and cannot get free.
9 My eyes grow weak because of oppression.
I call out to you, O LORD, all day long;
I spread out my hands in prayer to you.
10 Do you accomplish amazing things for the dead?
Do the departed spirits rise up and
give you thanks? (Selah)
11 Is your loyal love proclaimed in the grave,
or your faithfulness in the place of the dead?
12 Are your amazing deeds experienced in the dark region,
or your deliverance in the land of oblivion?
13 As for me, I cry out to you, O LORD;
in the morning my prayer confronts you.
14 O LORD, why do you reject me,
and pay no attention to me?
15 I am oppressed and have been on the
verge of death since my youth.
I have been subjected to your horrors
and am numb with pain.
16 Your anger overwhelms me;
your terrors destroy me.
17 They surround me like water all day long;
they join forces and encircle me.
18 You cause my friends and neighbors
to keep their distance;
those who know me leave me alone in the darkness.

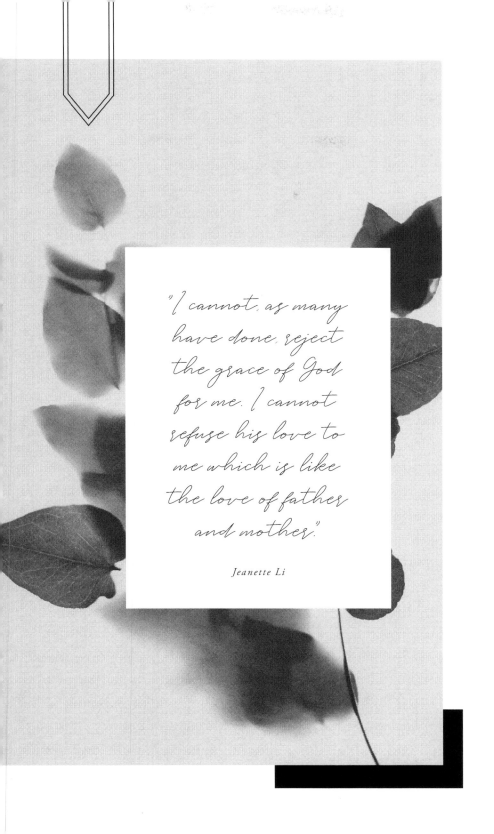

"I cannot, as many have done, reject the grace of God for me. I cannot refuse his love to me which is like the love of father and mother."

Jeanette Li

SOAP / *Psalm 88:13-14*
SCRIPTURE / *Write out the SOAP verses*

_____

_____

_____

_____

_____

_____

_____

_____

_____

_____

_____

_____

_____

_____

_____

_____

_____

_____

_____

_____

_____

_____

OBSERVATION / *Write 3 - 4 observations*

_____

_____

_____

_____

_____

_____

_____

APPLICATION / *Write down 1 - 2 applications*

PRAYER / *Write out a prayer over what you learned*

THANKFUL

*Write three things you are thankful for
today and why each one brings you joy.*

ONE

....
....
....
....
....
....
....

TWO

....
....
....
....
....
....
....

THREE

....
....
....
....
....
....
....

Psalm 89

A well-written song by Ethan the Ezrahite.

1 I will sing continually about the LORD's faithful deeds;
to future generations I will proclaim your faithfulness.
2 For I say, "Loyal love is permanently established;
in the skies you set up your faithfulness."
3 The LORD said,
"I have made a covenant with my chosen one;
I have made a promise on oath to David, my servant:
4 'I will give you an eternal dynasty
and establish your throne throughout
future generations.'" (Selah)
5 O LORD, the heavens praise your amazing deeds,
as well as your faithfulness in the angelic assembly.
6 For who in the skies can compare to the LORD?
Who is like the LORD among the heavenly beings,
7 a God who is honored in the great angelic assembly,
and more awesome than all who surround him?
8 O LORD God of Heaven's Armies!
Who is strong like you, O LORD?
Your faithfulness surrounds you.
9 You rule over the proud sea.
When its waves surge, you calm them.
10 You crushed the Proud One and killed it;
with your strong arm you scattered your enemies.
11 The heavens belong to you, as does the earth.
You made the world and all it contains.
12 You created the north and the south.
Tabor and Hermon rejoice in your name.
13 Your arm is powerful,
your hand strong,
your right hand victorious.
14 Equity and justice are the foundation of your throne.
Loyal love and faithfulness characterize your rule.
15 How blessed are the people who worship you!
O LORD, they experience your favor.
16 They rejoice in your name all day long,
and are vindicated by your justice.
17 For you give them splendor and strength.
By your favor we are victorious.

Psalm 89 (Continued)

18 For our shield belongs to the LORD,

our king to the Holy One of Israel.

19 Then you spoke through a vision to

your faithful followers and said:

"I have placed a young hero over a warrior;

I have raised up a young man from the people.

20 I have discovered David, my servant.

With my holy oil I have anointed him as king.

21 My hand will support him,

and my arm will strengthen him.

22 No enemy will be able to exact tribute from him;

a violent oppressor will not be able to humiliate him.

23 I will crush his enemies before him;

I will strike down those who hate him.

24 He will experience my faithfulness and loyal love,

and by my name he will win victories.

25 I will place his hand over the sea,

his right hand over the rivers.

26 He will call out to me,

'You are my father, my God, and the protector who delivers me.'

27 I will appoint him to be my firstborn son,

the most exalted of the earth's kings.

28 I will always extend my loyal love to him,

and my covenant with him is secure.

29 I will give him an eternal dynasty,

and make his throne as enduring as the skies above.

30 If his sons reject my law

and disobey my regulations,

31 if they break my rules

and do not keep my commandments,

32 I will punish their rebellion by beating them with a club,

their sin by inflicting them with bruises.

33 But I will not remove my loyal love from him,

nor be unfaithful to my promise.

34 I will not break my covenant

or go back on what I promised.

35 Once and for all I have vowed by my own holiness,

Psalm 89 (Continued)

I will never deceive David.
36 His dynasty will last forever.
His throne will endure before me, like the sun;
37 it will remain stable, like the moon.
His throne will endure like the skies." (Selah)
38 But you have spurned and rejected him;
you are angry with your chosen king.
39 You have repudiated your covenant with your servant;
you have thrown his crown to the ground.
40 You have broken down all his walls;
you have made his strongholds a heap of ruins.
41 All who pass by have robbed him;
he has become an object of disdain to his neighbors.
42 You have allowed his adversaries to be victorious,
and all his enemies to rejoice.
43 You turn back his sword from the adversary,
and have not sustained him in battle.
44 You have brought to an end his splendor,
and have knocked his throne to the ground.
45 You have cut short his youth,
and have covered him with shame. (Selah)
46 How long, O Lord, will this last?
Will you remain hidden forever?
Will your anger continue to burn like fire?
47 Take note of my brief lifespan.
Why do you make all people so mortal?
48 No man can live on without experiencing death,
or deliver his life from the power of Sheol. (Selah)
49 Where are your earlier faithful deeds, O Lord,
the ones performed in accordance with
your reliable oath to David?
50 Take note, O Lord, of the way your servants are taunted,
and of how I must bear so many insults from people.
51 Your enemies, O Lord, hurl insults;
they insult your chosen king as they dog his footsteps.
52 The Lord deserves praise forevermore!
We agree! We agree!

Psalm 90

A prayer of Moses, the man of God.

1 O Lord, you have been our protector
through all generations.
2 Even before the mountains came into existence,
or you brought the world into being,
you were the eternal God.
3 You make mankind return to the dust,
and say, "Return, O people."
4 Yes, in your eyes a thousand years
are like yesterday that quickly passes,
or like one of the divisions of the nighttime.
5 You bring their lives to an end and they "fall asleep."
In the morning they are like the grass that sprouts up:
6 In the morning it glistens and sprouts up;
at evening time it withers and dries up.
7 Yes, we are consumed by your anger;
we are terrified by your wrath.
8 You are aware of our sins;
you even know about our hidden sins.
9 Yes, throughout all our days we
experience your raging fury;
the years of our lives pass quickly, like a sigh.
10 The days of our lives add up to seventy years,
or eighty, if one is especially strong.
But even one's best years are marred
by trouble and oppression.
Yes, they pass quickly and we fly away.
11 Who can really fathom the intensity of your anger?
Your raging fury causes people to fear you.
12 So teach us to consider our mortality,
so that we might live wisely.
13 Turn back toward us, O Lord.
How long must this suffering last?

Psalm 90 (Continued)

Have pity on your servants.

14 Satisfy us in the morning with your loyal love.

Then we will shout for joy and be happy all our days.

15 Make us happy in proportion to

the days you have afflicted us,

in proportion to the years we have experienced trouble.

16 May your servants see your work.

May their sons see your majesty.

17 May our Sovereign God extend his favor to us.

Make our endeavors successful.

Yes, make them successful.

SOAP / *Psalm 89:32*
SCRIPTURE / *Write out the SOAP verses*

_____

_____

_____

_____

_____

_____

_____

_____

_____

_____

_____

_____

_____

_____

_____

_____

_____

_____

_____

_____

_____

OBSERVATION / *Write 3 - 4 observations*

_____

_____

_____

_____

_____

_____

APPLICATION / *Write down 1 - 2 applications*

PRAYER / *Write out a prayer over what you learned*

THANKFUL

WEEK 1 • FRIDAY

*Write three things you are thankful for
today and why each one brings you joy.*

ONE

....
....
....
....
....
....
....

TWO

....
....
....
....
....
....
....

THREE

....
....
....
....
....
....
....

REFLECT

Record an application you learned from your SOAP study this week and how you will practically implement it in your life.

....
....
....
....
....
....
....
....
....
....
....
....
....
....
....
....
....
....
....
....
....
....
....
....
....

Sing to the Lord a new song. Sing to the Lord, all the earth. Sing to the Lord. Praise his name. Announce every day how he delivers. Tell the nations about his splendor. Tell all the nations about his amazing deeds.

Psalm 96: 1-3

PRAY

*Write down your prayer requests
and praises for this week.*

....

....

....

....

....

....

....

....

....

....

....

....

....

....

....

....

....

....

....

....

....

....

....

....

....

....

....

....

Psalm 91

1 As for you, the one who lives in the shelter of the Most High,
and resides in the protective shadow of the Sovereign One—
2 I say this about the Lord, my shelter and my stronghold,
my God in whom I trust—
3 he will certainly rescue you from the snare of the hunter
and from the destructive plague.
4 He will shelter you with his wings;
you will find safety under his wings.
His faithfulness is like a shield or a protective wall.
5 You need not fear the terrors of the night,
the arrow that flies by day,
6 the plague that stalks in the darkness,
or the disease that ravages at noon.
7 Though a thousand may fall beside you,
and a multitude on your right side,
it will not reach you.
8 Certainly you will see it with your very own eyes—
you will see the wicked paid back.
9 For you have taken refuge in the Lord,
my shelter, the Most High.
10 No harm will overtake you;
no illness will come near your home.
11 For he will order his angels
to protect you in all you do.
12 They will lift you up in their hands,
so you will not slip and fall on a stone.
13 You will subdue a lion and a snake;
you will trample underfoot a young lion and a serpent.
14 The Lord says,
"Because he is devoted to me, I will deliver him;
I will protect him because he is loyal to me.
15 When he calls out to me, I will answer him.
I will be with him when he is in trouble;
I will rescue him and bring him honor.
16 I will satisfy him with long life,
and will let him see my salvation."

Psalm 92

A psalm; a song for the Sabbath day.

1 It is fitting to thank the LORD,
and to sing praises to your name, O Most High.
2 It is fitting to proclaim your loyal love in the morning,
and your faithfulness during the night,
3 to the accompaniment of a ten-stringed instrument and a lyre,
to the accompaniment of the meditative tone of the harp.
4 For you, O LORD, have made me happy by your work.
I will sing for joy because of what you have done.
5 How great are your works, O LORD!
Your plans are very intricate!
6 The spiritually insensitive do not recognize this;
the fool does not understand this.
7 When the wicked sprout up like grass,
and all the evildoers glisten,
it is so that they may be annihilated.
8 But you, O LORD, reign forever.
9 Indeed, look at your enemies, O LORD.
Indeed, look at how your enemies perish.
All the evildoers are scattered.
10 You exalt my horn like that of a wild ox.
I am covered with fresh oil.
11 I gloat in triumph over those who tried to ambush me;
I hear the defeated cries of the evil foes who attacked me.
12 The godly grow like a palm tree;
they grow high like a cedar in Lebanon.
13 Planted in the LORD's house,
they grow in the courts of our God.
14 They bear fruit even when they are old;
they are filled with vitality and have many leaves.
15 So they proclaim that the LORD, my Protector,
is just and never unfair.

JOURNAL
your thoughts

....
....
....
....
....
....
....
....
....
....
....
....
....
....
....
....
....

SOAP / *Psalm 91:15*
SCRIPTURE / *Write out the SOAP verses*

_____

_____

_____

_____

_____

_____

_____

_____

_____

_____

_____

_____

_____

_____

_____

_____

_____

_____

_____

OBSERVATION / *Write 3 - 4 observations*

_____

_____

_____

_____

_____

_____

_____

APPLICATION / *Write down 1 - 2 applications*

PRAYER / *Write out a prayer over what you learned*

THANKFUL

*Write three things you are thankful for
today and why each one brings you joy.*

ONE

....
....
....
....
....
....
....

TWO

....
....
....
....
....
....
....

THREE

....
....
....
....
....
....
....

Psalm 93

1 The LORD reigns.
He is robed in majesty.
The LORD is robed;
he wears strength around his waist.
Indeed, the world is established; it cannot be moved.
2 Your throne has been secure from ancient times;
you have always been king.
3 The waves roar, O LORD,
the waves roar,
the waves roar and crash.
4 Above the sound of the surging water,
and the mighty waves of the sea,
the LORD sits enthroned in majesty.
5 The rules you set down are completely reliable.
Holiness aptly adorns your house, O LORD, forever.

Psalm 94

1 O LORD, the God who avenges!
O God who avenges, reveal your splendor.
2 Rise up, O judge of the earth.
Pay back the proud.
3 O LORD, how long will the wicked,
how long will the wicked celebrate?
4 They spew out threats and speak defiantly;
all the evildoers boast.
5 O LORD, they crush your people;
they oppress the nation that belongs to you.
6 They kill the widow and the resident foreigner,
and they murder the fatherless.
7 Then they say, "The LORD does not see this;
the God of Jacob does not take notice of it."
8 Take notice of this, you ignorant people.
You fools, when will you ever understand?
9 Does the one who makes the human ear not hear?
Does the one who forms the human eye not see?

Psalm 94 (Continued)

10 Does the one who disciplines the nations not punish?
He is the one who imparts knowledge to human beings!
11 The LORD knows that peoples' thoughts
are morally bankrupt.
12 How blessed is the one whom you instruct, O LORD,
the one whom you teach from your law,
13 in order to protect him from times of trouble,
until the wicked are destroyed.
14 Certainly the LORD does not forsake his people;
he does not abandon the nation that belongs to him.
15 For justice will prevail,
and all the morally upright will be vindicated.
16 Who will rise up to defend me against the wicked?
Who will stand up for me against the evildoers?
17 If the LORD had not helped me,
I would soon have dwelt in the silence of death.
18 If I say, "My foot is slipping,"
your loyal love, O LORD, supports me.
19 When worries threaten to overwhelm me,
your soothing touch makes me happy.
20 Cruel rulers are not your allies,
those who make oppressive laws.
21 They conspire against the blameless,
and condemn to death the innocent.
22 But the LORD will protect me,
and my God will shelter me.
23 He will pay them back for their sin.
He will destroy them because of their evil;
the LORD our God will destroy them.

"A life totally committed to God has nothing to fear, nothing to lose, nothing to regret."

Pandita Ramabai

SOAP / *Psalm 94:12-13*
SCRIPTURE / *Write out the SOAP verses*

_____

_____

_____

_____

_____

_____

_____

_____

_____

_____

_____

_____

_____

_____

_____

_____

_____

_____

_____

OBSERVATION / *Write 3 - 4 observations*

_____

_____

_____

_____

_____

_____

_____

APPLICATION / *Write down 1 - 2 applications*

PRAYER / *Write out a prayer over what you learned*

THANKFUL

WEEK 2 · TUESDAY

Write three things you are thankful for today and why each one brings you joy.

ONE

....
....
....
....
....
....
....

TWO

....
....
....
....
....
....
....

THREE

....
....
....
....
....
....
....

Psalm 95

1 Come, let us sing for joy to the LORD.

Let us shout out praises to our Protector who delivers us.

2 Let us enter his presence with thanksgiving.

Let us shout out to him in celebration.

3 For the LORD is a great God,

a great king who is superior to all gods.

4 The depths of the earth are in his hand,

and the mountain peaks belong to him.

5 The sea is his, for he made it.

His hands formed the dry land.

6 Come, let us bow down and worship.

Let us kneel before the LORD, our Creator.

7 For he is our God;

we are the people of his pasture,

the sheep he owns.

Today, if only you would obey him.

8 He says, "Do not be stubborn like they were at Meribah,

like they were that day at Massah in the wilderness,

9 where your ancestors challenged my authority,

and tried my patience, even though

they had seen my work.

10 For forty years I was continually

disgusted with that generation,

and I said, 'These people desire to go astray;

they do not obey my commands.'

11 So I made a vow in my anger,

'They will never enter into the resting

place I had set aside for them.'"

Psalm 96

1 Sing to the LORD a new song.
Sing to the LORD, all the earth.
2 Sing to the LORD. Praise his name.
Announce every day how he delivers.
3 Tell the nations about his splendor.
Tell all the nations about his amazing deeds.
4 For the LORD is great and certainly worthy of praise;
he is more awesome than all gods.
5 For all the gods of the nations are worthless,
but the LORD made the sky.
6 Majestic splendor emanates from him;
his sanctuary is firmly established and beautiful.
7 Ascribe to the LORD, O families of the nations,
ascribe to the LORD splendor and strength.
8 Ascribe to the LORD the splendor he deserves.
Bring an offering and enter his courts.
9 Worship the LORD in holy attire.
Tremble before him, all the earth.
10 Say among the nations, "The LORD reigns!
The world is established; it cannot be moved.
He judges the nations fairly."
11 Let the sky rejoice, and the earth be happy.
Let the sea and everything in it shout.
12 Let the fields and everything in them celebrate.
Then let the trees of the forest shout with joy
13 before the LORD, for he comes.
For he comes to judge the earth.
He judges the world fairly,
and the nations in accordance with his justice.

A little
while, we are
in eternity;
before we find
ourselves there,
let us do much
for Christ.

Ann Hasseltine Judson

SOAP / *Psalm 96:1-3*
SCRIPTURE / *Write out the SOAP verses*

_____

_____

_____

_____

_____

_____

_____

_____

_____

_____

_____

_____

_____

_____

_____

_____

_____

_____

_____

_____

_____

_____

OBSERVATION / *Write 3 - 4 observations*

_____

_____

_____

_____

_____

_____

_____

APPLICATION / *Write down 1 - 2 applications*

PRAYER / *Write out a prayer over what you learned*

THANKFUL

*Write three things you are thankful for
today and why each one brings you joy.*

ONE

....
....
....
....
....
....
....

TWO

....
....
....
....
....
....
....

THREE

....
....
....
....
....
....
....

Psalm 97

1 The LORD reigns.
Let the earth be happy.
Let the many coastlands rejoice.
2 Dark clouds surround him;
equity and justice are the foundation of his throne.
3 Fire goes before him;
on every side it burns up his enemies.
4 His lightning bolts light up the world;
the earth sees and trembles.
5 The mountains melt like wax before the LORD,
before the LORD of the whole earth.
6 The sky declares his justice,
and all the nations see his splendor.
7 All who worship idols are ashamed,
those who boast about worthless idols.
All the gods bow down before him.
8 Zion hears and rejoices,
the towns of Judah are happy,
because of your judgments, O LORD.
9 For you, O LORD, are the Most High over the whole earth;
you are elevated high above all gods.
10 You who love the LORD, hate evil!
He protects the lives of his faithful followers;
he delivers them from the power of the wicked.
11 The godly bask in the light;
the morally upright experience joy.
12 You godly ones, rejoice in the LORD.
Give thanks to his holy name.

Psalm 98

A psalm.

1 Sing to the LORD a new song,
for he performs amazing deeds.
His right hand and his mighty arm
accomplish deliverance.
2 The LORD demonstrates his power to deliver;
in the sight of the nations he reveals his justice.
3 He remains loyal and faithful to the family of Israel.
All the ends of the earth see our God deliver us.
4 Shout out praises to the LORD, all the earth.
Break out in a joyful shout and sing!
5 Sing to the LORD accompanied by a harp,
accompanied by a harp and the sound of music.
6 With trumpets and the blaring of the ram's horn,
shout out praises before the king, the LORD.
7 Let the sea and everything in it shout,
along with the world and those who live in it.
8 Let the rivers clap their hands!
Let the mountains sing in unison
9 before the LORD.
For he comes to judge the earth.
He judges the world fairly,
and the nations in a just manner.

JOURNAL
your thoughts

....
....
....
....
....
....
....
....
....
....
....
....
....
....
....
....
....

SOAP / *Psalm 96:1-3*
SCRIPTURE / *Write out the SOAP verses*

_____

_____

_____

_____

_____

_____

_____

_____

_____

_____

_____

_____

_____

_____

_____

_____

_____

_____

_____

_____

OBSERVATION / *Write 3 - 4 observations*

_____

_____

_____

_____

_____

_____

APPLICATION / *Write down 1 - 2 applications*

PRAYER / *Write out a prayer over what you learned*

THANKFUL

*Write three things you are thankful for
today and why each one brings you joy.*

ONE

....
....
....
....
....
....
....

TWO

....
....
....
....
....
....
....

THREE

....
....
....
....
....
....
....

Psalm 99

1 The Lord reigns!
The nations tremble.
He sits enthroned above the cherubim;
the earth shakes.
2 The Lord is elevated in Zion;
he is exalted over all the nations.
3 Let them praise your great and awesome name.
He is holy!
4 The king is strong;
he loves justice.
You ensure that legal decisions will be made fairly;
you promote justice and equity in Jacob.
5 Praise the Lord our God.
Worship before his footstool.
He is holy!
6 Moses and Aaron were among his priests;
Samuel was one of those who prayed to him.
They prayed to the Lord and he answered them.
7 He spoke to them from a pillar of cloud;
they obeyed his regulations and the ordinance he gave them.
8 O Lord our God, you answered them.
They found you to be a forgiving God,
but also one who punished their sinful deeds.
9 Praise the Lord our God!
Worship on his holy hill,
for the Lord our God is holy.

Psalm 100

A thanksgiving psalm.

1 Shout out praises to the LORD, all the earth!
2 Worship the LORD with joy.
Enter his presence with joyful singing.
3 Acknowledge that the LORD is God.
He made us and we belong to him,
we are his people, the sheep of his pasture.
4 Enter his gates with thanksgiving,
and his courts with praise.
Give him thanks.
Praise his name.
5 For the LORD is good.
His loyal love endures,
and he is faithful through all generations.

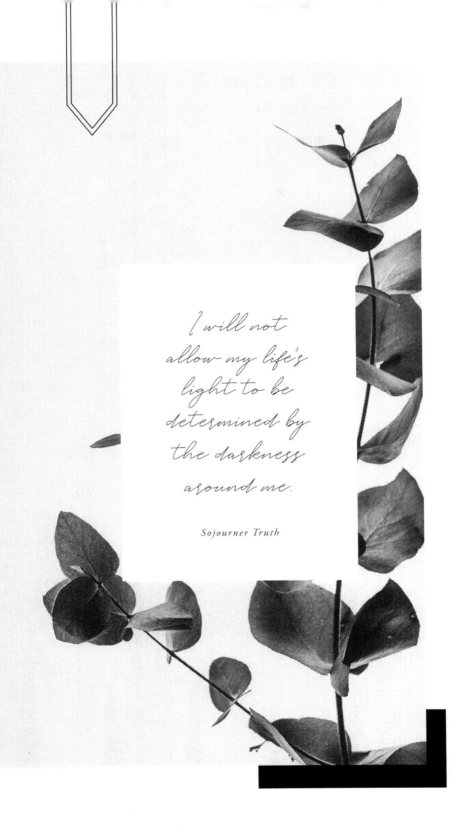

I will not allow my life's light to be determined by the darkness around me.

Sojourner Truth

SOAP

WEEK 2 · FRIDAY

SOAP / *Psalm 100:5*
SCRIPTURE / *Write out the SOAP verses*

_____

_____

_____

_____

_____

_____

_____

_____

_____

_____

_____

_____

_____

_____

_____

_____

_____

_____

_____

_____

_____

_____

OBSERVATION / *Write 3 - 4 observations*

_____

_____

_____

_____

_____

_____

_____

APPLICATION / *Write down 1 - 2 applications*

PRAYER / *Write out a prayer over what you learned*

THANKFUL

*Write three things you are thankful for
today and why each one brings you joy.*

ONE

....
....
....
....
....
....
....

TWO

....
....
....
....
....
....
....

THREE

....
....
....
....
....
....
....

REFLECT

Record an application you learned from your SOAP study this week and how you will practically implement it in your life.

....
....
....
....
....
....
....
....
....
....
....
....
....
....
....
....
....
....
....
....
....
....
....
....
....

Join Us

ONLINE
lovegodgreatly.com

JOURNALS
lovegodgreatly.com/store

FACEBOOK
lovegodgreatly

INSTAGRAM
@lovegodgreatlyofficial

APP
Love God Greatly

....

CONTACT US
info@lovegodgreatly.com

CONNECT
#LoveGodGreatly

FOR YOU

What we offer

30+ Translations
Bible Reading Plans
Online Bible Study
Love God Greatly App
Over 200 Countries Served
Bible Study Journals
Community Groups
Love God Greatly Bible
Love God Greatly Journal

Each study includes

Three Weekly Blog Posts
Daily Devotions
Memory Verses
Weekly Challenges
Weekly Reflection Questions
Bridge Reading Plan

Other studies

The Gospel of Mark
Everlasting Covenant
Jesus Our Everything
Know Love
Empowered: Yesterday and Today
Risen
Draw Near
Beatitudes
Esther
Words Matter
Walking in Victory
To Do Justice, To Love Kindness, To Walk Humbly
Faithful Love
Choose Brave
Savior
Promises of God
Love the Loveless
Truth Over Lies
1 & 2 Thessalonians
Fear & Anxiety
James

His Name Is...
Philippians
1 & 2 Timothy
Sold Out
Ruth
Broken & Redeemed
Walking in Wisdom
God With Us
In Everything Give Thanks
You Are Forgiven
David
Ecclesiastes
Growing Through Prayer
Names of God
Galatians
Psalm 119
1st & 2nd Peter
Made For Community
The Road To Christmas
The Source Of Gratitude
You Are Loved